An Antebellum
Plantation Household

An Antebellum Plantation Household

Including the South Carolina Low Country
Receipts and Remedies of Emily Wharton Sinkler

Anne Sinkler Whaley LeClercq

University of South Carolina Press

© 1996 University of South Carolina

Published in Columbia, South Carolina, by the
University of South Carolina Press

Manufactured in the United States of America

00 99   5   4

Library of Congress Cataloging-in-Publication Data

LeClercq, Anne Sinkler Whaley, 1942–
    An antebellum plantation household : including the South Carolina
low country receipts and remedies of Emily Wharton Sinkler / Anne
Sinkler Whaley LeClercq.
        p.   cm.
    Includes index.
    ISBN 1-57003-129-0
    1. Plantation life—South Carolina—Santee River Region—
History—19th century—Sources.   2. Santee River Region (S.C.)—
History—Sources.   3. Sinkler, Emily Wharton, 1823–1875—
Manuscripts.   4. Plantation owners' spouses—South Carolina—Santee
River Region—Manuscripts.   I. Sinkler, Emily Wharton, 1823–1875.
II. Title.
F277.S28L4   1996
975.7'8—dc20   96 9970

Contents

Contents

Contents

Introduction

In writing *An Antebellum Plantation Household: Including the South Carolina Low Country Receipts and Remedies of Emily Wharton Sinkler,* I hoped to convey some of the fascination I experienced as I read the intimate writings of an intrepid, humorous, lovely lady, Emily Wharton Sinkler. I read her letters and her receipt book (*receipt* is a low country variant of *recipe*) looking for the small details of life that might show how her days passed, whom she loved and whom she disliked, and what she thought about religion, politics, and slavery.

Emily Wharton Sinkler's letters to her family in Philadelphia and her receipt book are a treasure trove for finding the patina of her life. Emily Wharton Sinkler was a pioneer. She was born into a cultivated, prominent Philadelphia family in 1823. Her father, Thomas I. Wharton, was a noted lawyer and jurist. He served on the board of the American Philosophical Society, one of the first subscription libraries in the country. Her mother, Arabella Griffith, was raised at Charlies Hope—a plantation on the Delaware River. Arabella's mother, Mary Core Griffith, wrote novels and stories and spent over $25,000 on her apiary. The Whartons lived at 150 Walnut Street in the heart of old Philadelphia. They were Episcopalians and attended Christ Church, where patriots, loyalists, and heroes of the American Revolution had worshiped. Philadelphia in the antebellum years was a cultural center where art, theater, music, and publishing thrived. It was a commercial port of significance with imports from France, Italy, and Britain. It was a craft center without peer, with silversmiths, furniture makers, carriage shops, and more.

At the age of nineteen Emily married Charles Sinkler and moved eight hundred miles away to the swampy, low country region of Upper Saint John's Parish, an isolated area of cotton plantations on the Santee River in South Carolina. In Upper Saint John's Parish there were twenty-two plantations located in the alluvial land along the Santee River, just off Nelson's Ferry Road, and the River Road. The Sinklers were of Scotch descent, and the brothers James and Peter were the first Sinklers to settle in Upper Saint John's Parish.

When Emily arrived in Upper Saint John's Parish, her father-in-law, William Sinkler, owned four plantations on the Santee River: The Eutaw, Belvidere, Wampee, and Apsley. The pineland town of Eutawville with its sandy hills provided a summer retreat from malaria for these plantations' owners. The parish church was the Rocks Church. While the Sinklers were of Scotch ancestry, the other families—Porchers, Gaillards, Mazycks, Palmers, Ravenels, Cordeses, Marions, Dwights, and Gourdins—were French Huguenot. The area was isolated, accessible to Charleston, which was sixty miles away, either by barge on the Santee River or, after 1833, by railroad from a station at Branchville, some twenty miles by cart or carriage from Belvidere.

The Sinkler family had lived in Upper Saint John's Parish since 1785 when Capt. James Sinkler of Revolutionary War fame and his wife Margaret Cantey Sinkler moved from Lower Saint John's Parish, where they had been rice and indigo farmers, and built Belvidere Plantation. James's brother Peter Sinkler joined Gen. Francis Marion's rebel forces and was betrayed to the British by his brother-in-law, James Boisseau. Peter Sinkler witnessed the destruction of the following property before being led away to prison: "twenty thousand pounds of indigo, one hundred and thirty head of cattle, one hundred and fifty-four head of sheep, two hundred head of hogs, three thousand bushels of grain, twenty thousand rails, and household furniture valued at 2,500 pounds; in addition to which the British carried off 55 negroes, 16 blood horses, and 28 mares and colts."[1]

The French Huguenots had come to Upper Saint John's after the revocation of the Edict of Nantes in 1685 and found in the somber beauty of the Santee Swamp, with its forest walls of oak and cypress, an area inhab-

---

1. Harriette Kershaw Leiding, *Historic Houses of South Carolina* (Philadelphia: J. B. Lippincott Company, 1921), p. 133.

ited only by wild animals and widely separated villages of Santee Indians. A map of Upper Saint John's Parish from 1865 has this inscription: "Here dwelt a people in peace and contentment, whose ancestors had fled from tyranny in other lands. They tilled the ground and roamed the forests and at last, all was well with their world."[2] Saint John's Parish had been incorporated by the Church Act of 1706, and the settlement around Nelson's Ferry and Eutawville was known as Upper Saint John's Parish.

The Sinklers were avid hunters, expert farmers, and devoted horse racers. Charles's father, William Sinkler, owned 103 slaves, and Charles eventually farmed three cotton plantations and owned 195 slaves.[3] The marriage of Emily Wharton and Charles Sinkler was thus a mating of opposites: northern erudition and sophistication with rural, southern cotton plantation culture. This is not to say that Charles Sinkler was in the backwoods image of a Daniel Boone. Indeed, Charles had received his A.B. degree in 1835 from the College of Charleston, and along with twenty-eight other young men he gave a public oration, titled "On Eloquence," at a special "Exhibition" of the college on April 4, 1834.[4] Charles had joined the United States Navy as a midshipman in 1836. In 1842, while stationed in Philadelphia, he met and fell in love with the beautiful, petite Emily Wharton.

Emily's receipt book and her letters home to her Philadelphia family show how she made do in an environment that must have seemed unfamiliar, even strange, and presented many challenges. She invented alternatives for everyday necessities that had been readily available in Philadelphia. She learned how to manage a large plantation. She learned how to prepare remedies for the sick. Emily's writings show that she successfully combined Philadelphia culture and culinary traditions with those of Upper Saint John's Parish.

Using these two primary sources, Emily's letters and her receipt book,

---

2. Map, 1865, no title. A copy of this map is owned by this author.

3. Chalmers G. Davidson, *The Last Foray, The South Carolina Planters of 1860: A Sociological Study* (Columbia: University of South Carolina Press, 1971), pp. 149–50.

4. Davidson, *The Last Foray*, p. 22.

I hoped to depict everyday life in the antebellum low country of South Carolina. My intent was to be unobtrusive, letting Emily speak for herself. But I have done this with the knowledge that I am selecting bits and pieces from Emily's past in creating a picture of her daily routines.

The transcriptions of Emily's receipt book and the portrait of Emily from her letters were undertaken in the belief that they reveal much about the conditions of life on an antebellum plantation in low country South Carolina. Emily's receipt book shows the significant role of the caretaker, generally women in the antebellum South, to the health and hygiene of the plantation population. Emily was responsible for husbanding the provisions grown on the plantation so that the population of over two hundred persons would have food, clothing, household supplies, and medical remedies throughout the year. This was quite an undertaking at a time when the nearest stores were in Charleston and there was no refrigeration or electricity. Emily relied on salt for curing meat and pickling for preservation of perishable vegetables and fruits. The receipts show that locally grown ingredients were meticulously measured and used: cornmeal, rice, mutton, beef, wheat flour, pork, butter, eggs, and milk. Imported ingredients were few: sugar, salt, and some seasonings such as nutmeg, mace, curry, and ginger.

Writing Letters Home

Emily wrote many letters home to Philadelphia to her father, Thomas I. Wharton; to her mother, Arabella Griffith Wharton; to her older sister, Mary; and to her two brothers, Henry and Frank. There are sixty-seven letters written from 1842 to 1857. Transcriptions of those letters were placed in the South Caroliniana Library at the University of South Carolina in Columbia by Laura Anne Sinkler Manning, the daughter of Mary Sinkler Stevens, who was the fourth child of Emily Wharton Sinkler and Charles Sinkler. The original letters were found in 1996 among the papers of Anne Sinkler Fishburne. There is a single copy of a letter in the hand of Emily Wharton Sinkler dated 1865. It is located in the Sinkler Papers at the South Carolina Historical Society in Charleston.

The letters provide a flavorful record of plantation cooking, food preparation, travel anecdotes, country and city friendships, and much more.

The portrait of Emily that emerges from the letters is that of a fun-loving, well-read, multilingual individual with avid interests including gardening, singing, church work, sewing, and embroidery. Emily was fluent in French, Italian, and German, reading Johann Wolfgang von Goethe and Friedrich von Schiller in German. She sang the songs of the "Swedish Nightingale," Jenny Lind, as well as the operas of Gaetano Donizetti and Gioacchino Rossini. She was an avid reader, enjoying the contemporary authors of her time such as Washington Irving, Charles Dickens, and Charlotte Brontë. Emily had a keen eye for observing life around her, and an infectious sense of humor.

The letters are a month by month record of Emily's life at the Sinkler plantations, The Eutaw and Belvidere. They also provide a record of Emily's life at Woodford, a Sinkler summer retreat in the sandhills at Bradford Springs, South Carolina. Emily visited frequently in Charleston and Philadelphia, and her accounts of teas, dances, races, operas, and other city fun enliven her letters. She had many Charleston and Columbia friends. She visited Mrs. Hampton in Columbia and stayed with the James Simonses and Henry Lesesnes in Charleston. She shopped on King Street, purchasing mantillas, flowers, and hair combs. She particularly loved the February excitement of the races at the Washington Race Track that were sponsored by the South Carolina Jockey Club.

Emily's letters reflect the vibrancy and wealth of the low country during the crucial years of the 1840s and 1850s, when plantation society was at its peak of power and wealth. Charles Sinkler farmed at least three cotton plantations during this time, and his ownership of 195 slaves is an indication of his wealth. Emily's letters cast a new perspective on this period in low country history. They show her concern with slave laws that prohibited education of slaves and plantation customs that allowed the separation of slave families. Emily Wharton Sinkler was a woman of her times. She graced the Sinklers' plantations with her Philadelphia sophistication and charm and was indeed the "light and joy" of Belvidere. She became a low country mistress of a cotton plantation, enjoying the challenges of country life and the gaiety of city visits.

Writing the Receipt Book

Emily's receipt book, begun in Charleston in 1855, was written and handed down from Emily Wharton Sinkler to her daughter-in-law, Anne

Wickham Porcher Sinkler. Internal evidence in the book indicates that Anne Wickham Porcher Sinkler added a number of her own receipts to the book. However, she used Emily's index and format. Anne's handwriting is different from that of Emily, and she wrote in pencil.

The receipt book was handed down from Anne Wickham Porcher Sinkler to her daughter Anne Sinkler Fishburne, who also used the receipt book, making many of her own additions. Anne Sinkler Fishburne's receipts call for ingredients not available to her mother and grandmother, such as gelatin instead of Coopers Isinglass, and baking soda for Soda Saleratus. Anne Sinkler Fishburne carried grandmother Emily's receipt book with her when Belvidere, the home plantation of the Sinklers since 1785, was engulfed in 1940 by the waters of the Santee-Cooper Project that created Lake Marion and Lake Moultrie. Anne copied many of the recipes from the receipt book into her self-published "Old Receipts from Old Saint John's." Anne Fishburne lived for many years on her beautiful thirteen-acre farm in Pinopolis, South Carolina, where the receipt book was kept and used. When my grandmother Anne Sinkler Fishburne died in 1981, her lovely house was emptied of its furniture, books, and paintings. Sad to say, but the next generation had no one who wanted to take on the cares of a small farm in rural South Carolina. Among the treasures discovered was the receipt book.

The book is brittle due to the acidity of the paper on which it was written, and also because of the acid paste used to attach household remedies gathered from local news sources. The binding is worn, and in places the ink is blurred so that deciphering the writing is difficult. Emily's receipt book has a number of paste-ins. She cut out recipes and home remedies from an array of newspapers. Here she describes the scene at The Eutaw where all are reading papers sent by the Whartons: "Who thought of sending me the *Ladies Register*? It is the very thing I wanted. Do you know it contained the most charming receipts which Eliza and I are going to try."[5]

---

5. Emily Wharton Sinkler to Thomas I. Wharton (father), December 29, 1842. Sinkler Letters, South Caroliniana Library, University of South Carolina, Columbia, S.C. [All letters in this publication, unless otherwise noted, are from the Sinkler Letters at the South Caroliniana Library.]

Emily's receipts show the influences of French Huguenot cooking, of low country rice culture, of the Virginia use of cornmeal in breads and spoon breads, and of her own northern traditions of cooking with potatoes and wheat and buckwheat flour. Her receipts also reflect the African American slave cooking traditions such as flavoring soups and vegetables with salt pork, deep-frying meats, and using hominy and cornbread. Emily's use of macaroni and vermicelli shows a distinct Italian influence.

Emily's sources for her food receipts were many: the cooks at Belvidere and The Eutaw such as Chloe, Rachel, and Satira; her low country neighbors such as the Gaillards, Porchers, and Mannings to whom she attributed many of her receipts; her sister, Mary Wharton, who sent her German receipts from the Philadelphia newspapers; her best friend and sister-in-law, Elizabeth Sinkler (Eliza), who managed the house at The Eutaw; and her Columbia friend Mary Cantey Hampton, whom she mentions as the source of her charlotte russe recipe.[6]

Emily speaks of having a French cookbook given her by Seaman Deas Sinkler, her brother-in-law, and undoubtedly she had other contemporary cookbooks, such as Sarah Rutledge's *The Carolina Housewife*, first published in 1847, and Mary Randolph's *The Virginia House-wife*, first published in 1824. Emily attributes several of her receipts to a Mrs. Randolph, and there is no reason to believe that they were not those by Mary Randolph. Several of the Mary Randolph receipts are: "Vermicelli," "Salad Dressing," "Cosmetic Soap," "To Make Soap," and "Old Fowl Soup."[7] Emily frequently served vermicelli soup, and the receipt most assuredly came from *The Virginia House-wife*. Many of Emily's receipts have the same names as those in Sarah Rutledge's *The Carolina Housewife*, such as "Indian Cakes," "White Fricassee," "Sauce Piquante," "Potatoes a la Lyonnaise," "Maitre d'Hotel Potatoes," "Charlotte of Apples," "Plum Pudding," and "Sweet

---

6. Mary Cantey Hampton (1780–1863) was the daughter of John Cantey and in 1801 married Wade Hampton of Columbia, S.C.

7. Mary Randolph, *The Virginia House-wife, with Historical Notes and Commentaries by Karen Hess* (Columbia: University of South Carolina Press, 1984) and Sarah Rutledge, *The Carolina Housewife or House and Home by a Lady of Charleston* (Charleston: Walker, Evans & Cogswell, 1963).

Potato Pone." While Emily does not attribute these receipts to Miss Rutledge, one can assume, because of the similarity in ingredients and cooking style, that Emily owned a copy of *The Carolina Housewife.*

The book shows the meticulous nature of its original author. The frontispiece bears the name Emily Sinkler, the date 1855, and the place Charleston. An alphabetical index at the end carefully notes the page and name of each entry. The original book contained seven major sections: Meats (pages 1–6), Miscellaneous (pages 7–13), Vegetables (pages 14–24), Desserts (pages 25–42), Bread and Warm Cakes (pages 43–70); Miscellaneous (pages 71–90); and Medical Receipts (pages 91–106).

The reader will discover a trove of practical, resourceful, ingenious advice in each section. The Meats section shows the availability of low country game. There are receipts for duck stew and venison pastry. Belvidere had turkeys, chickens, sheep, and cows, and thus it is not surprising that there are receipts for roasting a turkey, making English mutton sausages, and using beef leftovers in stews and pies. Emily has two receipts for "Bouilli Beef," which use beef bouillon and meat stewed for many hours. Emily's "Beef Scrapple" combines the simmering of a beef bone with Indian meal to make a breakfast cake and is probably a concoction of one of her fine African American cooks.

The Vegetables section shows Emily's adeptness with pickling and preserving to make the most of seasonal tomatoes, for example, in soy, in ketchup, and put up in stone jars. In her letters Emily refers to spring asparagus and peas, but there are no recipes in her receipt book for preparing either of these fresh, though she does put asparagus into her pea soup. Emily used okra in "Okra a la Maulie," which combines okra and tomatoes with ham and onions, simmered for three hours to make a gumbo. She also used it in Julien Soup, Mrs. Paul.

Emily's Philadelphia heritage is evident in her extensive use of potatoes. There are over ten receipts for using potatoes in puddings, in bread, as cheese, as croquettes, and boiled. Emily used Irish potatoes, yams, and sweet "Spanish" potatoes.

Emily had a passion for desserts. She generally served three desserts as a finale to her dinner parties. There were puddings made from locally grown ingredients such as blackberries and plums, served with a wine or a "hard," sugar-based sauce. There were custards and creams made from sugar, cream, and eggs available on the plantation.

Emily's Bread and Warm Cakes section shows the influence of the traditional southern use of cornmeal and rice. Indian meal from ground corn was used in such warm spoon breads as "Bannocks," "Indian Cakes," and "Baked Indian Pudding," the last of which was sweetened with another local ingredient, molasses. The importance of southern rice culture, with its provenances and its African American adaptations, is seen in such specialties as "French Rice Pudding," "Rice Cakes," "Rice Scones," and "Rice Bread."

Emily also prepared remedies for all manner of diseases, from consumption to alcoholism. The careful selection of remedies shows a concern for the health and hygiene of an extended family. The low country was especially plagued by mosquito-born diseases such as malaria and yellow fever. Symptoms of the diseases were high fevers, chills, jaundice, and debilitation. Emily had remedies for catastrophic diseases such as typhoid and tetanus (lockjaw), and for the more mundane such as dysentery and sore throat. Many of her medical remedies relied on blackberry cordials and blackberry wines made at Belvidere.

Emily's sources for her medical remedies were her Upper Saint John's doctor, Dr. Francis Peyre Porcher, mentioned in her receipt book; and her Charleston doctors, Dr. Henry Rutledge Frost and Dr. Francis Kinloch Huger, mentioned in her letters.[8] She also had medical clippings from newspapers, as well as contemporary works such as that of Anne Cobbett. Indeed, Emily's receipt for "Bread Jelly for the Sick" is identical to one found in Cobbett's *English Housekeeper,* first published in 1851.

Pharmacy and the practice of medicine underwent significant changes

8. Joseph Ioor Waring, *History of Medicine in South Carolina, 1825–1900,* volume 2 (Columbia: Medical Association of South Carolina, 1967). Dr. Francis Peyre Porcher (1824–1895), son of Isabella Sarah Peyre and Dr. William Porcher, married first in 1855 to Virginia Leigh and second in 1877 to Margaret Ward. Dr. Henry Rutledge Frost (1795–1866) lived in Charleston. Not only was Dr. Francis Kinloch Huger (1773–1855) Emily's first doctor in Charleston, but his daughters, Elizabeth Pinckney Huger (1804–1882) and Harriet Horry Huger (1822–1857), became Emily's warmest friends in Charleston.

in the 1840s and 1850s. Pharmacists, chemists, and botanists made major discoveries in the 1850s that doctors soon employed in the practice of medicine. Alkaloids such as morphine, ipecac, narcotine, strychnine, and quinine were extracted as the active principles of plants. Glycosides, or sugars, from plants such as digitalis were discovered. Halogens, including chlorine and iodine, were derived from chemical compounds and became important in both medicine and sanitation. In Emily's day there were no antitoxins or vaccines to deal with such killing diseases as tetanus and diphtheria. Emily's medical remedies show that she was familiar with such plant-based ingredients as quinine, morphine sulfate, iodine sulfate, chloroform, chlorine, and strychnine. She also knew and used the chemical compounds of her day such as lead nitrate, potassium chlorate, lead iodide, iron iodide, potassium bromide, and iron sulfate. Emily's medical therapies are an amalgam of an earlier therapy consisting of strong cathartics, powerful emetics, enemas and bleeding, and an emerging set of medical therapies based on alkaloids, glycosides, and halogen compounds.[9]

Emily had numerous formulas for household remedies. She knew how to make hair wash and hair dye. She had concoctions for getting rid of stains on floors and in clothes and fine linens. The sources of her household remedies would be much the same as those for her food receipts: local newspaper clippings, the slaves at The Eutaw and Belvidere, and contemporary sources such as Anne Cobbett's *English Housekeeper.* Cobbett's book has many household remedies whose pattern Emily followed, as in Cobbett's "To Destroy Bugs," "Blacking for Shoes," and "To Take Oil from Stone or Boards." The ingredients used by Cobbett such as sweet oil, unslacked lime, pearl ash, rottenstone, silver caustic, gum arabic, and corrosive sublimate are all ingredients found in Emily's household remedies.[10]

The receipt book has been faithfully transcribed in terms of spelling. Emily's distinctive handwriting is a marvel of fine ink penmanship, which unfortunately cannot be saved in the transcription. Her unique *x* (two *c*'s

---

9. David L. Cowne and William H. Helfand, *Pharmacy, An Illustrated History* (New York: Harry N. Abrams, 1990), pp. 100–145.

10. Anne Cobbett, *English Housekeeper* (London: A. Cobbett, 1851), pp. 375–81.

back to back) is her own talisman. Her punctuation is very scant: no commas, very few periods, and much use of a single hyphen. This author has normalized the punctuation for ease of reading. Emily's spelling shows the British influence, as in using a *u* in *neighbour,* and she also capitalizes many nouns. These have not been changed. The newsprint additions have been transcribed in the order that they appear. The reader will recognize their appearance because they are noted with a dot. Emily faithfully attributes many receipts and remedies to her friends, neighbors, and doctors. This says a great deal about the social exchanges that must have taken place on Sundays in churches and at other gatherings.

An Antebellum Plantation Household is organized in two parts, reflecting the two primary source documents. Part I is a portrait of Emily's life at Belvidere drawn almost entirely from her letters but with footnotes that provide a context for life in the antebellum South. The letters provide the setting for Emily's receipts and remedies. Part II contains the receipt book. A glossary of unusual or unfamiliar terms is provided at the end of this section.

It is one of the small miracles of life that Emily's worn and much used receipt book should have survived the trauma of the flooding of Belvidere and been handed down, finally, to Anne Sinkler Whaley LeClercq, the author.

This book is dedicated to my husband Frederic Schumann Le Clercq, who has listened patiently to tales of Emily and the Sinklers. I am also deeply appreciative for the superb editorial assistance of Dr. Alexander Moore, Director of the South Carolina Historical Society.

I hope that *An Antebellum Plantation Household* will contribute to the circle of life those antebellum customs and traditions of the Sinkler family that might still have some meaning today.

Part I

*Portrait of
Emily Wharton Sinkler—
from Her Letters, 1842–1865*

Arriving in the South Carolina Low Country

Emily Wharton Sinkler arrived in low country South Carolina in 1842 as the bride of Charles Sinkler. She had been born in Philadelphia on October 12, 1823, and was only nineteen years old when she married Charles. A crayon portrait of Emily shows that she had lovely, wide, light blue eyes and wore her dark straight hair in the empire fashion of the day, pulled back and parted in the middle.[11] Emily loved the color blue, and when she asked for cloth from Philadelphia, she spoke of blue silk and blue cambric. She was small boned and petite and weighed only 104 pounds (letter, December 16, 1851).

Charles, born at The Eutaw in Upper Saint John's Parish on July 8, 1818, served in the United States Navy from 1836 to 1847. During that time he went on a three-year voyage on the USS *Columbia II* to China and the Orient, going around the Cape of Good Hope. He was stationed briefly upon his return in Philadelphia, and there he met Emily Wharton, the daughter of the eminent jurist Thomas I. Wharton and Arabella Griffith.[12] They were married in Philadelphia on September 8, 1842, and returned to the South, living with Charles's father, William Sinkler, at The Eutaw Plantation.

Living at The Eutaw

Emily missed her family over eight hundred miles away in Philadelphia: her brothers, Henry and Frank; her sister, Mary; and her "Mama" and "Papa." She begs for letters and scolds her brothers when none arrive. She was painfully homesick. She took yearly trips home to Philadelphia in

---

11. Anne Sinkler Fishburne, *Belvidere: A Plantation Memory* (Columbia: University of South Carolina Press, 1949), p. 44.

12. *American Philosophical Society Proceedings,* volume 22, part 3, Minutes, 1744–1838 (Philadelphia: McCalla & Stavely, 1885). Thomas I. Wharton was elected to membership in the American Philosophical Society in 1830 and was partly responsible in 1835 for having gas lights installed in the library. The American Philosophical Society was founded in 1743 by Benjamin Franklin and is the oldest learned society in the United States.

the summer, but without telephones and photographs, memories and letters were her principal solace for homesickness, until the daguerreotype was developed. Emily writes about the new invention, photography: "Take Papa down to Langenheims with all possible secrecy and have his Daguerre taken exactly like yours for me. Be sure to do this for then I will have the whole family except Hen [her brother Henry] and he I expect soon to see in *propria persona*" (letter, December 10, 1847).

At The Eutaw Plantation when Emily arrived in 1842, the lady in charge of housekeeping was Elizabeth Allen Sinkler (Eliza to Emily), the sister of Emily's husband, Charles Sinkler. Elizabeth was considered an excellent cook, and her influence is felt in Emily's receipt book with the many references to Elizabeth's receipts. There were eight adults in residence at The Eutaw. There was the *beau pere,* Emily's father-in-law, William Sinkler. Emily never mentions her mother-in-law, Elizabeth Allen Broun Sinkler, and that was because she had died on June 3, 1824. Charles's living brothers were James Sinkler, Dr. Seaman Deas Sinkler, and William Henry Sinkler. He had one sister, Elizabeth Allen Sinkler (Eliza). Emily and Charles moved into The Eutaw with the beau pere, William Henry Sinkler and his wife Anna, James Sinkler and his wife Margaret, and Eliza.

The Eutaw was a large frame house with big central rooms, a front hall, two side extensions, large piazzas, and big double chimneys. It had only four bedrooms. As was typical of a plantation house in Upper Saint John's, it was high off the ground on six substantial brick arches. The Eutaw was located on the River Road and was approximately four miles from Eutawville. It was connected to Belvidere by a foot bridge over the Santee Swamp and Eutaw Creek.

Emily was startled at the number of house servants at The Eutaw. She describes them as getting in the way of each other: "Housekeeping is very different at the South from the North though I think one thing is, people here give themselves too much trouble about it and have a great many too many servants about the house which of course creates great confusion. For instance there are but four bedrooms to be attended to in the house and there are five chambermaids to attend to them, so of course that makes just five times as much confusion as is necessary" (letter, February 11, 1843).

The Eutaw was a thriving cotton plantation[13] farmed by the beau pere, as Emily called her father-in-law. Emily describes produce that included corn, potatoes, and oats: "By the bye this neighbourhood is making excellent crops of cotton and our little place with only 10 hands to work it makes 900 dollars. The beau pere has just put up four thousand bushels of corn, six thousand bushels of potatoes, six hundred of oats."[14]

William Sinkler and his sons were serious farmers, always looking for the newest inventions to make their lands profitable. Emily's letters have several references to new ploughs that were being purchased in Philadelphia and shipped south. In the spring of 1847 the Sinklers entertained several agricultural experts who had come to advise them on new ways to fertilize crops:

We have had two men at work this week with whom you would have been delighted. They came to show some new plan of making manure and stayed several days. They were Frenchmen and from the part near Switzerland. One was a hussar in Napoleon's army for many years and served four years in Germany, Battle of Austerlitz, etc. He is a real character and says he left France the day Louis Bonaparte

---

13. Harold D. Woodman, *Slavery and the Southern Economy, Sources and Readings* (New York: Harcourt, Brace & World, 1966), pp. 5–11. Long-staple cotton had been an important cash crop for the islands of South Carolina from the end of the eighteenth century. However, it was not until the invention of the cotton gin by Eli Whitney in 1793 that the growing of short-staple cotton on the interior lands of the state became feasible. In the 1780s South Carolina and Georgia grew 2 million pounds. They grew 30 million pounds by 1801, and by 1860 over 4.5 million bales, each averaging 450 pounds, were grown in the South. Southern cotton became the nation's number one export.

14. Emily Wharton Sinkler to Thomas I. Wharton (father), November 15, 1845. The beau pere had immense land holdings in Upper Saint John's, much of it prime cotton farm land and the remainder pinelands. William Sinkler, "Will of William Sinkler," in Charleston Co. Wills (WPA typescript), vol. 46A, 1851–1856, pp. 292–96, in Charleston Co. Library. When William Sinkler died in 1856, he left 103 slaves to his three sons. He left James Sinkler two tracts of land, Brackey and Brushpond. He left Charles Sinkler Belvidere and four hundred acres of swampland adjoining Belvidere. He left William Henry Sinkler The Eutaw. He left Charles and William Henry the plantation called Dorcher.

was exiled, and will never return until he is on the throne. I talked French and German to him. I suppose you will raise your eyes and say what sort? But at any rate he thought it wonderful.[15]

South Carolina had a strong French connection, both because French was the dominant European culture in the early nineteenth century and because of the large number of Huguenots in South Carolina. Emily's language is full of French expressions. Her letters are peppered with: *comme il faut, au fait, d'oyley, in statu quo,* "I have not the *de quoi,*" "but *que voulez vous,*" "apropos," "the utmost *sang froid,*" *conseil de famille,* and many more.

Meals at The Eutaw were plentiful, leisurely, and served three times a day. Emily continued her Philadelphia custom of eating wheat toast for breakfast but watched with amazement as her new family breakfasted on hotcakes, waffles, biscuits, and hominy, the last of which was totally new to her:

> Perhaps you would like to know how we spend our days. Breakfast is from half past eight to quarter to nine. I get up at seven. Mr. Sinkler five mornings out of seven gets up at four or five and mounts a horse and goes off to shoot English wild ducks or deer or foxes. All the family assemble at nine thirty for family prayers. There is a great variety of hot cakes, waffles, biscuits. I don't take to all these vanities however and always eat toast for breakfast and supper. They make excellent wheat bread and toast it very nicely by the coals. Hominy is a most favourite dish. They eat it at all their meals. It is what is called grits in Philadelphia. We take breakfast in the hall and sit there all the morning. Soon after breakfast our little carriage comes to the door and we set off to take a drive. The whole equipage is quite *comme il faut.* The carriage is perfectly plain just holding two persons. The horses are very dark brown with plain black harness. When we set out the dogs come running up so we have a cortege of two greyhounds and two terriers generally. We are always proceeded by Sampson on horseback to open gates. We are home at twelve or one and I then read and sew until dinner time. We dine between three and four. Eliza is an excellent housekeeper, and the ice cream here is really the best I ever tasted. We have supper at half past eight which is very much like breakfast except we have cold meat and after the cloth is removed wine and cordials. In the evening we have music, both piano and guitar. (letter, December 5, 1842)

---

15. Emily Wharton Sinkler to Mary Wharton, May 13, 1847. Emily spoke French and German and sang Italian. This author has Emily's French grammar book, *Collot's Progressive French,* which is underlined and shows hard use.

Emily's first Christmas at Eutaw was a glorious occasion. She describes the breakfast festivities thus: "Before breakfast everyone takes a glass of egg-nogg, and a slice of cake. It is the universal custom and was not on this occasion omitted by anybody. As Christmas was kept five days egg-nogg was regularly drank every morning" (letter, December 29, 1842).

The Eutaw was located just off the Santee swamps, where swarms of malaria-carrying mosquitoes made life impossible from May to October. Thus the extended Sinkler family were in residence at The Eutaw only from the first killing frost in October through the end of May. For the four summer months they went to the Sinklers' pineland house in Eutawville.[16] When Emily was not at the Sinkler house in Eutawville, she spent her summers at their house in Bradford Springs, South Carolina, at a rented house on Sullivan's Island, South Carolina, or in the mountains of North Carolina at Flat Rock. Each year she made a voyage home to Philadelphia.

Living at Belvidere

In January of 1848 Emily and Charles Sinkler moved the short distance across Eutaw Springs to Belvidere. Belvidere, like The Eutaw, was in Upper Saint John's Parish, and it was located on the cypress- and oak-lined Santee River. Capt. James Sinkler, son of a Scotch immigrant, secured a land grant to Belvidere in 1770. In 1785 the Belvidere house was built by Captain Sinkler's wife, Margaret Cantey Sinkler. However, in 1808 William Sinkler, Emily's father-in-law and the son of Capt. James Sinkler, built The Eutaw, and Belvidere remained uninhabited until Emily and Charles moved back there in 1848. At Belvidere Emily was the mistress of a large house, family, and an extended family of, eventually, over 195 slaves.

Belvidere was a prosperous cotton plantation. Charles would, in time,

---

16. Eutawville was a pineland village about two miles from The Eutaw and Belvidere. The village was located on sandy hills, making it relatively safe from malaria during the summer months. Many of the old summer houses remain, giving the area a historic feel. The Eutaw Springs Battle Field of Revolutionary War fame is located just at the edge of town.

amass over a thousand acres, all called Belvidere but consisting of five individually named tracts: Dorshee, Black Jack, Brackee, Belvidere, and a small piece of The Eutaw.[17] Belvidere was shaped like a huge piece of pie with the north rim running along the Santee River, the southwest boundary along Eutaw Creek, and the southeast boundary marked by the River Road. It was bisected by Nelson's Ferry Road.

Farming was an often precarious undertaking with success dependent on unpredictable markets and equally unpredictable weather.[18] Charles, who had spent his twenties in the navy, became an accomplished farmer who diversified his planting to include not only cotton but also corn, wheat, and vegetables, in season. He undoubtedly learned farming from his father, the beau pere. Emily speaks frequently of his concern for the weather and his crops: "So as Charles' corn is calling loudly for work he cannot spare the beasts from the ploughs for two or three days and I must bear the disappointment" [of not getting the mail earlier] (letter, May 21, 1850). And in another letter we see Emily's sense of humor: "The weather is quite warm enough to satisfy any reasonable person, planters and farmers not included of course. For those worthy individuals incorporate themselves so thoroughly in the feelings of their crops that instead of enjoying the cool nights and mornings and a blanket at night they are thinking of the shivering cotton which tho it warms others unfortunately cannot warm itself" (letter, May 30, 1850).

Emily first mentions Belvidere in a January 1848 letter. She is obviously excited to be "arranging everything to my taste" and having her own house after living with her in-laws for six years. The furniture for Belvidere

---

17. J. P. Gaillard, *Map Showing the Santee Cooper Project South of Santee River. Showing the Plantations proposed to be flooded in the Santee Reservoir,* May 1, 1942. Reproduced in part in Illustrations.

18. Woodman, *Slavery and the Southern Economy,* pp. 46–47. Some have questioned whether raising cotton with slave labor was profitable. On a plantation of fifty slaves in 1850 it is estimated that the planter received only $880 in profits. If this average farm produced 158 bales of cotton at 10 cents a pound, the cash income would be $6,320, while the expenses would come to $5,440 calculated as interest on each slave, depreciation in slave property, annual hire of an overseer, purchase of slave clothing, and plantation supplies. The capital investment in fifty slaves, each costing approximately $600, was thus $30,000.

had been given by the Whartons and had been shipped from Philadelphia, which was a center for fine furniture making in the nineteenth century: "Fortunately there was not one shower during the whole transportation which was not to have been expected as they came from Philadelphia in separate detachments, then came up the Santee in an open canal boat and were then waggoned thirteen miles. It is too hard that after giving everything you and Mama can not see how handsome all looks."[19]

Housekeeping at Belvidere was a new experience for Emily, and she describes it in some detail. Emily set up housekeeping at Belvidere with Charles, her husband, and her three young children, Elizabeth Allen (Lizzie), Wharton (Bud), and Arabella (Ella), all of whom had been born while she lived at The Eutaw. She had three house servants. Emily's remarks show that she was well aware that she lived in the backwoods:

> One occurrence I must relate tho it savours a little of life in the backwoods. The servants consist of Bull, waiter and coachman, Rachel, chambermaid and washerwoman and Chloe, cook. The first two have been with us for a long while and are quite *au fait* to everything but the latter has only been learning to cook for a short time and knows very little of genteel manners. One day I gave her a piece of Delaware herring by way of a treat to cook for tea but to my horror three or four minutes after I gave it to her I heard a tramp approaching and enter Chloe smiling with the fish broiled, it being five in the afternoon. I gave her some partridges, which she inquired were to be thrown out. (letter, January 17, 1848)

Visitors to Belvidere from surrounding plantations, from Philadelphia, and from Charleston were many. They were a special treat breaking the isolation of day-to-day living. Emily describes the anticipation of arriving visitors: "On Tuesday we dined at Wampee[20] and on Wednesday had a bridal visit from Mr. and Mrs. Keating Simons who stopped on their way to Chickasaw, his place where we intend dining next week. We have had

---

19. Emily Wharton Sinkler to Thomas I. Wharton, January 3, 1848. Begun in 1793 and opened in 1801, the Santee Canal was designed by Col. Christian Senf, a Swedish engineer. It was a thirty-five-foot-wide, twenty-two-mile-long ditch with twelve locks and eight aqueducts. The canal connected Charleston via the Cooper River to the Santee River.

20. Wampee was owned by Emily's brother-in-law, James Sinkler, and was about five miles south of Belvidere.

several visitors last week which is an event in the country, when we are sitting in the hall to hear it exclaimed, there is a carriage coming up the avenue, and the conjectures etc" (letter, December 10, 1842). On another occasion Emily describes the custom of going and staying a week or more with friends: "I spent a short time in Columbia most delightfully with Mrs. Manning. The people there are the most hospitable I ever saw and I have made all sorts of promises for visits this winter. People here think no more of asking you to spend a week with them than you would in Philadelphia of inviting to tea" (letter, October 7, 1844).

In almost every letter Emily pleads with members of her family to visit. She particularly adored her fun-loving brother Henry. Among Emily's first visitors at Belvidere was Henry, whom she describes with obvious delight as "amiable, agreeable, gentlemanly, handsome, intelligent, in fine all he should be."

The Sinklers were much into horse racing. There was a race track at The Eutaw with regular races sponsored by the Upper Saint John's Jockey Club. Not only did the Sinklers train their own horses but neighbors sent their horses for training. Silver goblets with inscriptions for the winning horses still exist today. The wind vane at Belvidere spun a copper jockey in racing silks on horseback. The races were one of the principal social events of both the country and the city. Emily writes home that Henry is to go to the Charleston races, which were a yearly February event where Charleston blue bloods and country plantation owners mixed and mingled.[21] Horses and riding were definitely a new experience for Emily, and she shows some disdain for the family's adoration of horseflesh: "It is ridiculous the care

---

21. *Charleston Daily Courier*, February 2 and 12, 1853, p. 3. The February races were put on by the South Carolina Jockey Club and were held at the Washington Race Course, which is located in the area of Hampton Park today. The races lasted for four days. The price of admission was $2.50 for an omnibus and 10 cents for each passenger, while a buggy and pair cost 75 cents, a person on foot 10 cents, and a saddle horse 25 cents. The Jockey Club also hosted an annual dinner at the Saint Andrews' Hall for members, and on the last day of the races the Jockey Club put on the Jockey Club Ball there. Other festive events in February included the Saint Cecilia Society Ball, also held at the Saint Andrews' Hall, and the Military Ball of the Washington Light Infantry, held at Military Hall.

they take of them. Each horse has two boys to take care of him and a groom to take care of all of them. The horses eat the most dainty food and have to be rubbed with whiskey and actually drink it too. Every day before they take exercise they eat twenty eggs" (letter, February 6, 1843).

The beau pere, William Sinkler, always had several horses racing in the Charleston February races and generally did very well in the money: "Do not be alarmed about his [Henry] going to the races. It is an entirely different affair from the Northern Races, no gambling and all the ladies go. The beau pere has a horse to run for whom he was offered the other day $2,500."[22] Emily describes this horse in a later letter: "The races begin tomorrow and last for three days. The Charleston races begin next week. They have sent five horses from the stables here, only one however belongs to Eutaw, the rest are sent to be trained. Jeanette Berkeley is the name of the horse. She is going to run both here and in Charleston and they think she has a good chance" (letter, February 6, 1843).

Exactly ten years later the beau pere again had a horse entered in the Charleston races, a favorite named Jeff Davis. Emily was undoubtedly at the races, enjoying the crowds and the festivity associated with this event: "He [the beau pere] was successful at the Races one day. 'Jeff Davis,' his famous horse, beat the four-mile day, but [he, the beau pere] was disappointed about a favourite horse with which he had taken great pains and which was rulled out, i.e. not allowed to run because the rider had forgotten to put on his belt of shot to make him even in weight with the other riders" (letter, February 8, 1853).

Belvidere was a cotton plantation but was self-sufficient in terms of corn, rice, flour, poultry, mutton, and vegetables, in season. But sugar, coffee, salt, fruits, and candy were available only in Charleston. Thus the boxes of store-bought goodies as well as such things as napkin rings, sent by the Philadelphia Whartons to Emily, were events and treasured treats.

---

22. Emily Wharton Sinkler to Thomas I. Wharton, February 16, 1848. The equivalent of $2,500 would be approximately $25,000 today. The most recent cost of living indexes show that one 1842 dollar equaled ten dollars in 1982–1984. Standard & Poor's Corporation, *Standard & Poor's Trade & Securities. Statistics* (New York: Standard & Poor Corporation, 1994), p. 76.

Emily describes a box that included a chair, raisins (to be kept for "great occasions"), apples ("much relished by the children who have had none for a long while"), a white box of bonbons (some looking exactly like real strawberries), "Gaiter boots," coffee, napkin rings, an almanac for Charles, and sugar plums (letter, March 27, 1848).

Belvidere must have been truly glorious in the spring with the elm trees blossoming and, as Emily describes, crab apple trees in bloom: "This is the time to see the south. I am sitting now with the door open and a crab apple tree directly in front is laden with blossoms diffusing the most delightful fragrance through the whole air. The only spring thing we have is asparagus as yet but our green peas tho not in blossom are a foot high" (letter, March 27, 1848). Emily was much taken with the sweet olive, noting that "the perfume is enchanting and it will stay out the whole winter."[23]

The original garden at Belvidere had been designed and planted by Capt. James Sinkler's wife, Margaret Cantey Sinkler. When they died Belvidere remained uninhabited until Charles and Emily moved there from The Eutaw in 1848. Emily thus inherited a garden whose shape and design had been established but that was overgrown and in need of new planting. Emily obviously enjoyed this task and wrote home to her family about the excitement of establishing her own garden: "I wish I had you [Henry] here to consult with. Charles has given me a carpenter to work under my direction for a month and a person to garden, so my hands are full. The old garden is to be restored. It is now nearly forty years since it was tended but it contains many shrubs yet. I have arranged a small garden on each side of the front steps which is to be inclosed with an iron fence and is to contain the choicest speciments." Emily goes on to tell of the roses and

---

23. Emily Wharton Sinkler to Mary Wharton, November 14, 1847. George Macdonald Hocking, *A Dictionary of Terms in Pharmacognosy and Other Divisions of Economic Botany* (Springfield, Ill.: Charles C. Thomas, Publisher, 1955), s.v. "Calycanthus." The sweet olive blooms in winter and early spring in the low country, perfuming the air. It is of the species *olea fragrans* and is today commonly called the tea olive.

perennials she expects to plant: "I have already some very fine roses which have taken so well that they will bloom this spring. The Glory of France, Harrisonian de Brunnius, Cloth of Gold, and Souvenir de Malmaison. This last is the most splendid rose you ever saw, as large as a coffee cup and so firm and rich. I am foraging all through the country for roots and cuttings" (letter, February 23, 1852).

Emily was fascinated with gardening, scouring the countryside for cuttings and root clippings.[24] The garden at Belvidere with its beautiful iris walk and its rose hedges was the creation of Emily and her able African American gardeners. She collected plants from her friends and neighbors: "On Saturday we paid a visit to old Mrs. Marions, an old lady who lives at some distance from here and who is celebrated for her Garden. It is worth seeing. The thousands of bulbous roots all in full flower made it look very gay. I supplied myself well with roots and cuttings of different plants. One thing I know you would think pretty is the Rose Hedge. It is of the Daily Rose which is green here all through the winter. It is kept cut and trimmed to a certain size and is the most luxuriant thing you can imagine. I am planning one here" (letter, March 8, 1852).

Emily also ordered seeds from Philadelphia for her Belvidere garden, and her lovely annual and perennial borders are a family legend: "I enclose 12 cents in this letter and wish you would buy me a paper of the best mignonette seed and also a paper of Heart's Ease seed of the large dark purple sort. There is a variety in which the petals are large and dark and there is only a small spot of bright yellow in the middle" (letter, November 30, 1848). Emily received gifts of plants from friends, as acknowledged here: "I received this week some very fine rose trees, Cloth of Gold, Souvenir de Malmaison etc., a present from a gentleman we met at the Tournament last year" (letter, December 16, 1851).

---

24. Emily's fascination with gardening was based on an extensive knowledge of botany. Her copy of *North American Botany; Comprising the Native and Common Cultivated Plants North of Mexico*, by Amos Eaton and John Wright, published in 1840 by Elias Gates in Troy, N.Y., is underlined and annotated. Dried herbs and flowers that Emily placed between pages are still there. It is owned by this author, Anne Sinkler LeClercq.

Of course, Belvidere was heated only by fireplaces; when it got cold in the South in winter the plantation could be truly unpleasant. Emily describes the weather in December of 1851:

> And such weather as we have had. The coldest known in this Latitude since 1835. I know you will scarcely believe me when I tell you that the Thermometer in our Piazza pointed to only 12. The change began on Tuesday night; it blew fearfully, and on Wednesday morning it began to snow. It snowed heavily all that day and it was not until Sunday night that the weather moderated at all. The snow remained on the ground for four days, an unusual thing here. The ice was so thick in my room that we could not break it and even in Eliza Manning's room where she kept a fire burning all night, the water froze hard. I assure you it was entirely too cold to be pleasant.[25]

In a spring letter Emily describes the weather as warm, without fires: "We are progressing here to a remarkably early Spring. Everything is looking green and leafy. Lilacs, Roses, and many other Spring things are in full bloom, and the only fear now is that there will come a cold snap and kill everything. We have actually not had a fire in the house since I last wrote, and it is so mild that we always keep a window open in the day. Among the Spring things, Shad have come. I do wish you could have some of the abundance. The beau pere sent out a fisherman on Friday who brought back eight and one on Saturday who brought four. All very fine ones too."[26]

Emily's days at Belvidere were taken up with reading, music, long walks, and horseback riding. Her activity, of course, depended on the weather, as she says here: "the weather has been delightful, just cold enough to make exercise out of doors very attractive and to make it necessary to have a fire in doors all day. *Faux de mieux* I have taken to riding Tackey again. Anna is coming over to stay here, and we intend delightful

---

25. Emily Wharton Sinkler to Thomas I. Wharton, December 22, 1851. Elizabeth Allen Sinkler (Eliza) had married Col. Richard Irvine Manning of Holmesly Plantation in March of 1845. Belvidere had wide, covered front and side verandas, which were called "piazzas" after the Italian word for town squares.

26. Emily Wharton Sinkler to Mary Wharton, March 15, 1852. Shad is a fresh-water salmon that lived in the Santee and still can be caught in Lake Moultrie and Lake Marion, which were formed by the damming of the Santee.

long rides every day, I on Tackey Anna on Camilla. Now if we only had you here to go on Jeanette how pleasant it would be."[27]

When Emily moved to Belvidere in January of 1848 she brought with her the three children, Lizzie, Wharton, and Ella, the latter two months old. Emily's letters home during that winter and into the spring are filled with maternal details: "I am now writing with the baby in my arms" (letter, January 31, 1848). "They [the children] all go out soon after break-fast and stay nearly all day, Little Ella sleeping in the basket wagon. That child is the sweetest creature you can imagine, very much like Lizzie both in size and face" (letter, March 27, 1848).

We next hear from Emily in November of 1848 [eight months later], and it is apparent, though unmentioned, that Ella has died. Emily makes no mention of Ella but does say, "how sick I am of mourning, it is the hottest dress in the world" (letter, November 30, 1848). Perhaps because of Ella's death during the summer, undoubtedly of one of the dread diseases such as malaria or diphtheria, the Sinkler family made a major decision and purchased a summer place near Bradford Springs, South Carolina, in the Santee Hills, which they called Woodford. Emily used this new home as an added inducement in trying to get her Philadelphia family to visit: "This is an additional reason for your coming this winter to see how you like Wood-ford. The beau pere is to live with us half the year there and Brother James is thinking of buying a place very near for a summer residence. So the Sinkler family have made up their minds to be no more wanderers and pilgrims for six months of the year" (letter, November 30, 1848).

Retreating to Bradford Springs, to Woodford[28]

Emily seemed to be quite happy at Woodford and was delighted to be close to her favorite sister-in-law, Eliza, who had married Col. Richard I.

---

27. Emily Wharton Sinkler to Mary Wharton, January 12, 1852. Anna Sinkler, married to William Henry Sinkler, was Emily's sister-in-law and lived at The Eutaw. Ladies did not ride astride at this time, so the three friends would have gone riding sidesaddle and would have worn divided sidesad-dle skirts.

28. Woodford was the residence of Isaac Wharton from 1793 to 1808, and Emily probably visited

Manning and lived nearby (letter, February 21, 1850). Emily and Charles joined the Episcopal church at Bradford Springs, and Charles became a warden of the church. Bradford Springs was a sandhills retreat, similar in purpose to Flat Rock, North Carolina, or Sullivan's Island, off the coast of Charleston. It was located just south of Camden and just north of State-burg. There was a railroad line connecting Branchville to Stateburg, so Emily and her family may have gone between Belvidere and Bradford Springs by train. However, she speaks of crossing the Santee swamp in ferries on her trips between Belvidere and Bradford Springs.

In her first summer at Woodford, her neighbors the Gaillards' house burned down, and the whole family, including five children with whooping cough, came to Woodford to stay with the Sinklers for two weeks. Emily describes the scene as pandemonium: "The five children all with whooping cough, the nurses, etc, our small house with but two spare rooms, Rachel, my main dependence, sick, and the fact of all the little blackeys headed by Roberty, never having had the disease" (letter, May 21, 1850). Emily knew that they would be quarantined, as a result of the sickness, from all neighbors, and life would be more isolated than ever.

While at Woodford in the summer of 1850, which Emily describes as the hottest in thirty years with temperatures over ninety degrees every day, she received another one of those wonderful boxes of presents and necessities that the Whartons sent her regularly from Philadelphia. The box contained books for all members of the family, newspapers, bonbons from Henriades and Olivers, ginger lozenges from Browns, *"Papeterie"* (one of Emily's Frenchisms for stationery), "beautiful dresses, a lovely scarf, so *comme il faut* and so delicate, so different from the Charleston Mantillas," a parasol, ribbons, collars, cuffs, gloves and boots, hats for all, and more (letter, May 27, 1850).

For the Woodford house Emily had plans to order a piano, but she was given one, a Chickering, by the Gaillards, whom the Sinklers had be-

---

this lovely brick house in the Philadelphia environs on many occasions. Perhaps Emily decided to name her place in the Santee Hills after this family home. There is a picture of Isaac Wharton's Woodford in the Sinkler Papers in the South Carolina Historical Society, in Charleston, S.C.

friended at the time of their house fire. Emily speaks of having wonderful fresh raspberries and having a great deal of company every day: "We had company to dinner, Friday the Nelsons, Saturday Mrs. Hummel, Tuesday Mr. Elliott and Mr. Wilkinson, Wednesday the Converses, Major Porcher and Mr. Manigault, and to day Mr. Adams and Mr. Gaillard."[29] The Gaillards brought an "immense basket of the finest fruit of various sorts," which was a great treat as "the worms have destroyed all ours" (letter, August 8, 1850). Emily is no longer pleading for letters from home, and it is apparent that she is quite busy with managing the place, entertaining guests, and responding to her huge circle of letter writers: "I received twenty-two letters in July and of course they all had to be answered" (letter, August 8, 1850).

Reading and Singing

Emily's life at The Eutaw and at Belvidere was a cycle of the seasons, with lovely warm, long falls lasting into December. Activity centered around children, planting, housekeeping, reading, and singing. Without telephones, or television, newspapers from Charleston and Philadelphia were the only source of world events. Emily's letters are full of pleas for Saturday editions of the Philadelphia paper, the *Recorder,*[30] for old copies of the *Illustrated News,* for music from opera to simple duets for herself and Anna to sing, and for books by authors such as Dickens and Brontë. Each year she subscribed to a Philadelphia paper, the *Recorder:* "If still some money remains I will be much obliged if Henry will subscribe to the *Recorder* for another year immediately as I think it must be almost a year since he subscribed last for us" (letter, January 3, 1848). Emily's family sent her copies of the Philadelphia newspaper *The Ledger* on a regular basis.

Charleston had one of the first subscription libraries in the country,

---

29. Because Bradford Springs was a summer retreat for low country South Carolina, Emily's friends at Woodford were from all parts of the state: the Manigaults were from Charleston; the Gaillards and Porchers were from Upper Saint John's Parish; the Elliotts and Nelsons were from the Columbia area; and the Adamses were from Fort Mott.

30. *The Philadelphia Register and National Recorder,* Philadelphia, 1819–

the Charleston Library Society.[31] In 1847 Emily describes her excitement at joining this society: "We have succeeded in having a share in the Charleston Library which has slumbered in the family since it was founded, transferred to us and I can get as many books out as I want. The Librarian told Mr. Sinkler that he would find the Library a pleasant lounge in the morning, which he was not particularly gratified to hear as you know he likes to sit in a corner with a book and neither speak to nor look at any one" (letter, October 24, 1847).

Emily was an avid reader, as was Charles. Emily describes their book collection at Belvidere as numbering over six hundred volumes. "The Encyclopedia are very useful, hardly a day passes but we refer to them for something. You would be surprised to see how many valuable books we have; we have nearly 600 books. Some we had before but the most valuable belonged to poor Seaman [Charles's deceased younger brother] and some are beautifully bound. We have nearly all the standard works" (letter, February 16, 1848). Emily yearned for new books but relied on the old standards when she was without. As she says in one letter: "I have seen no new books for ten months and am now reading over Irving's works but he is such a favourite of mine that I never get tired of reading his books."[32]

Almanacs were a principal source of information for weather and crop projections in the nineteenth century. Charles, as a farmer, was interested in almanacs and magazines about farming, several of which he had sent

---

31. Jane H. Pease and William H. Pease, "Intellectual Life in the 1830's: the Institutional Framework and the Charleston Style," in *Intellectual Life in Antebellum Charleston,* edited by Michael O'Brien and David Moltke-Hansen (Knoxville: University of Tennessee Press, 1986), p. 149. The Charleston Library Society was established in 1748 and from 1835 occupied the old Bank of South Carolina building at Broad and Church. Its collections and comfortable reading room are still enjoyed today on a subscription basis. It was "more a gentlemen's preserve than a bibliophiles' retreat. . . . Their library grew from about 5,000 volumes in 1830 to 25,000 in 1848, strong in collections of literary and historical works and well stocked with volumes on political theory, philosophy, and natural science."

32. Emily Wharton Sinkler to Thomas I. Wharton, March 15, 1845. Emily is referring to Washington Irving, the famous American author of such works as *Rip Van Winkle, The Life of George Washington,* and *The Alhambra.* Irving wrote during the period 1832 to 1897 and was thus a contemporary of Emily's.

from Philadelphia. Here Emily is requesting that such be sent: "By the bye I had almost forgotten Mr. Sinkler wants Henry to subscribe 10 dollars for the *Cultivator* at Ziebers for this year 1846 and have it sent to Vances Ferry P.O." (letter, January 1, 1846). But Charles also read novels, as here: "Charles is delighted with his *Man of War* and on the strength of its having his name on the title page claims it as his own property in the Captain Cuttle way."[33]

News arrived by paper, or by friends, and thus subscriptions to newspapers were central to keeping informed about local and world events. Emily was anxious to hear Philadelphia news, national news, and even international news. As she says here: "When you are done with the *London News* do send them on. They are a great treat and go the rounds of the neighbourhood" (letter, February 28, 1846). She particularly liked the Saturday Philadelphia papers as they told who was getting married and other newsy details of her friends: "On Monday evening I received your letter, also one from Mary. The *Ladies Newspaper,*[34] a *Ledger*[35] is always acceptable" (letter, February 16, 1848).

Serialized novels were a customary form of light entertainment in the nineteenth century, and indeed most of Dickens's novels were first published in that fashion. Emily loved romances and light fiction and took umbrage at her sister's condescension to her reading tastes: *"En passant* how very cutting you are about my literary tastes. I would have you to know that I am rather more cultivated and enlightened in my tastes than you think. My scale is rather above *Leslie* etc.; *Life in Earnest*[36] I have read with a great deal of pleasure and have lent it to several persons. Tell Mama *Peranzabuloe* is delightful" (letter, February 11, 1847).

---

33. Emily Wharton Sinkler to Thomas I. Wharton, May 27, 1850. Emily is probably referring to William Thompson Townsend's *The Lost Ship or The Man of War's Man and the Privateer,* published first in 1843. Captain Cuttle was a fatherly, kind old ship's captain who befriended Florence Dombey and her dog Diogenes in Charles Dickens's 1846 *Dombey and Son.*

34. *Ladies Newspaper,* London, 1845–1851.

35. *Public Ledger,* Philadelphia, 1836– .

36. James Hamilton, *Life in Earnest* (London, 1845). The author has been unable to identify a bibliographic record for either *Leslie* or *Penanzabuloe.*

Dickens was on Emily's list, and she read many of his works in serialized form: "Thank Hen [Emily's brother Henry] for the *'Battle of Life.'* I had not read it before but I am very much disappointed in it. I think it is the poorest of Dickens works."[37] In a later letter she asks for the latest serialization of *Dombey:* "I see that a steamer has come and suppose there is a new *Dombey.* If so will you send it to me when every one is quite finished with it. If you will also send me *Neal* (oh call it weak not low) I shall be very grateful" (letter, October 24, 1847). And again when she has finished *Dombey* she is disappointed with it: "The last *Dombey* is just published here and I have read it. There is very little in it don't you think? So much sameness in all the characters. They are so extremely true to themselves the whole time that it is quite tiresome."[38]

Emily was an avid correspondent, and in each letter home she begs for Saturday newspapers from Philadelphia, books, and letters from her friends and family: "What new books have been lately imported by the city library? I am afraid you would think me sadly behind the age for I have not seen a new book since I left Philadelphia six months ago. We intended subscribing for the *Living Age*[39] in Charleston but I quite forgot it as we were coming off. If you ever buy any of the numbers do keep them for me, also any Saturday paper. Any thing of the kind is an excessive treat in the country" (letter, December 7, 1844).

Many evenings were spent reading aloud from the latest book. Many of the books were from the Whartons in Philadelphia, as here: "We are enjoying excessively the books which came in the box. *H. More*[40] we are reading together and like very much. I feel so intimate with the Johnson set that when we come to any complimentary allusion to him I feel as flattered and gratified as if it were to Frank or Hen. I have read *Sir Edward*

---

37. Emily Wharton Sinkler to Mary Wharton, March 18, 1847. Charles Dickens, *Battle of Life: A Love Story* (London: Bradbury & Evans, 1846; Boston: Redding, 1847).
38. Emily Wharton Sinkler to Mary Wharton, November 7, 1847. Charles Dickens, *Dombey and Son* (London, 1846).
39. *Littell's Living Age,* Boston, 1844–1896.
40. Hannah Moore, *H. Moore's Private Devotion* (Hartford: Brown & Parsons, 1845).

Graham[41] but am rather disappointed in it" (letter, May 30, 1850). On another occasion she asks what the Whartons are reading: "What are you reading now which is interesting? We are reading *Southey*[42] but it is not to be compared in point of interest to *Lockhart's Life*.[43] There is so much sameness and egotism about those letters" (letter, December 22, 1851).

Because there was no electricity, much reading must have been done around the fire in the dining and living rooms at Belvidere where there were also oil, and later gas, lamps. Emily kept up with the latest fiction as well as serious biography. Here she comments on Charlotte Brontë's *Jane Eyre:* "Have I ever told you how beautiful I think *Jane Eyre*?[44] How much superiour to *Dombey*.[45] Did you notice in the book some of the new styles of spelling in center, theater?" (letter, February 26, 1856).

Long, leisurely country days were spent not only with newspapers and books but with music. Family tradition has it that Emily had a beautiful soprano voice. She and her sisters-in-law, Eliza and Anna, were accomplished at the guitar and piano and in singing. Emily has not been long at The Eutaw when she speaks of a guitar: "The weather was lovely yesterday. Eliza and I took a long walk in the morning. It was so warm that we only wore our sunbonnets and no shawls. We were accompanied by two most interesting terriers and two grey hounds. Mr. Sinkler Sr. [the beau pere] returns from town to-morrow. He is going to bring up a guitar for Anna and myself" (letter, November 28, 1842).

Family singing, both in Italian and German, were festive occasions with Eliza at the piano and Emily and Anna singing. Emily had a special love for opera and frequently asked her sister Mary to go searching in Philadelphia for some particular piece of music: "Anna wants with the money that is left one of the opera books such as I bought at Carey and Harts. Mary knows the sort and can get it. She must get either *Anna Bolena*

---

41. Catherine Sinclair, *Sir Edward Graham* (London: Longman, Brown, Green & Longmans, 1849).

42. Robert Southey, *The Poetical Works of Robert Southey* (Paris: A. & W. Galignani, 1829).

43. J. G. Lockhart, *Lockhart's Life of Scott* (London, 1848).

44. Charlotte Brontë, *Jane Eyre* (London, 1847).

45. Charles Dickens, *Dombey and Son* (London, 1846–1848).

Puritani, La Muette di Portici or *Otello,* and if neither of these are to be had Mary can choose what she thinks best with the exception of *Norma* and *Somnambula.*"[46] In anticipation of her yearly trip home to Philadelphia, Emily practiced new songs for her family: "Anna and I are practicing two new duets for your especial edification. I hope you are getting ready some pieces which will suit the tastes of persons who are not quite *au fait* to intricate music. 'La Coupe' I know will be liked. By the bye did you get the music book I sent you by Dr. Huger and did you see him?"[47]

Emily's family were all musical. Philadelphia and New York were centers for the performing arts. Emily longed for full flesh-and-blood performances and is perhaps envious of her siblings' ability to be a part of exciting city life: "Oh Hen how I felt when I read that you had heard the Havanna Opera troupe in *Lucia.* Of all Operas I should prefer hearing that. Do you think you enjoyed the music sufficiently, Sir?" (letter, May 21, 1850).

The musical evenings at The Eutaw included guests from Charleston. Emily describes such an evening, revealing some distaste for sentimental music:

> Mr. Kinloch is up here now and I suppose will stay an indefinite time. He makes himself very pleasant and agreeable and is quite an addition to our little circle. In the evening we have some very good music. Anna and I have some nice new duets and Tom Kinloch has brought up his flute. To be sure he will harp on the heart's affections, the forsaken and twilight dews but every one is so used to his singing

---

46. Emily Wharton Sinkler to Thomas I. Wharton, December 6, 1845. Stephen LaRue, *International Dictionary of Opera* (Detroit: St. James Press, 1993). Gaetano Donizetti wrote *Anna Bolena Puritani* and *Lucia di Lammermoor;* Vincenzo Bellini wrote *Norma* and *La Somnambula;* D. F. E. Auber, a French musician, wrote *La Muette di Portici;* Gioacchino Rossini wrote *Otello. Anna Bolena Puritani* was first performed in Milan on December 26, 1830; *Lucia di Lammermore* was first performed in Naples on September 26, 1835; *Norma* was first performed on December 26, 1831, in Milan; while *La Somnambula* was first performed on March 16, 1833, in Venice. *La Muette di Portici* was first performed in Paris on February 29, 1828, and Rossini's *Otello* was first performed in Rome on January 25, 1817. It is interesting that Emily was singing quite contemporary operas.
47. Emily Wharton Sinkler to Mary Wharton, November 30, 1848. Emily refers to her friend and doctor, Dr. Francis Kinloch Huger (1773–1855). Dr. Huger's two daughters, Elizabeth Pinckney Huger (1804–1882) and Harriet Horry Huger (1822–1857), were among Emily's warmest Charleston friends.

them that it would not seem natural for him not to sing them every evening. Seaman [Charles's younger brother and a doctor in Charleston] has given Anna and myself each an opera (the music I mean) and I am determined this winter to practice so that when I come on I will surprise you. (letter, December 13, 1845)

Lizzie, Emily's oldest daughter, had wonderful memories of the musical evenings at The Eutaw: "Mamma and Aunt Anna entertained the guests in the drawing room by singing duets which sounded to me like the songs of angels. Their voices were so lovely and so well trained, one soprano and one contralto, and they were fascinated with Jenny Lind's songs of which they had a number."[48] Lizzie goes on to comment on Emily's guitar: "They each had a guitar with a blue ribbon, and sang Italian and German songs on moonlight evenings on the piazza, while the mocking birds only waited for pauses to trill out their liquid notes."[49]

There was a Steinway grand piano at both The Eutaw and Belvidere. Steinways were expensive even at that time, as they were imported from Hamburg, Germany. Here Emily is hoping for a new piano: "The beau pere has promised us a new piano this winter but I am afraid we will not get it for Seaman says he must buy one which he has seen in town and which costs 580 dollars and the beau pere says that 400 is quite enough."[50]

---

48. *The Baker Biographical Dictionary of Musicians, 8th ed.* (New York: Schirmer Books, 1992). Jenny Lind was born in Stockholm in 1820. Her real name was Johanna Maria Lind. She had a beautiful soprano voice with warm coloratura and a compass reaching high G. She was an established opera singer. She toured the United States in 1850 and 1851 giving ninety-three concerts, the final one of which was in Philadelphia. Her tour was sponsored by P. T. Barnum and was enthusiastically received by the American public, much like a rock star show of today. She sang in English, and Emily would have known many of her popular songs such as "Coming Through the Rye," "The Last Rose of Summer," and "John Anderson, My Joe." Thomas Edison's phonograph was not introduced in the United States until the 1870s, so Emily would have become familiar with Lind's songs either through sheet music or through performances.
49. Elizabeth Allen Coxe, *Memories of a South Carolina Plantation During the War* ("Privately Printed for My Family and Friends," n.p. 1912). Elizabeth Allen Coxe, as noted on the title page, was the "Daughter of Charles Sinkler of Belvidere." Lizzie notes that Emily's guitar had come from Spain, was inlaid with mother of pearl, and "was dashed to pieces by one of the negro soldiers during the raid at Belvidere."
50. Emily Wharton Sinkler to Mrs. Thomas I. Wharton, December 13, 1845. A $600 piano in 1845 would cost approximately $6,000 today. Standard & Poor's Corporation, *Standard & Poor's Trade & Securities. Statistics* (New York: Standard & Poor Corporation, 1994), p. 76.

Traveling by Carriage, Ship, and Train

Travel in low country South Carolina was fraught with perils such as potholed dirt roads, unpredictable ferries, noisy and dirty railroads, and steamship travel plagued with squalls and hurricanes. Both railroads and steamships were innovations of the 1830s and 1840s, and in their young years travel on them was frequently hazardous.

Emily was an intrepid traveler, thinking nothing of going by boat on stormy seas between Charleston and Philadelphia, or of making summer peregrinations "in her own conveyance," which had come from Philadelphia and cost two hundred dollars, between the watering springs of Virginia and low country South Carolina (letter, October 24, 1847). She regularly made the wagon plus train[51] trek from Vances Ferry, the mail post nearest The Eutaw and Belvidere, to the Branchville railroad station, and on to Charleston to the Lining Street station. Her letters are full of graphic accounts that touch on the perils of such travel by rail, schooner, and horse carriage. Indeed in her first letter home from Charleston she comments: "Every one congratulates us on the escape we had in the Wilmington boat. All who expected us were very much alarmed and thought the boat would never reach Charleston. It certainly did blow terribly."[52]

---

51. Samuel M. Derrick, *Centennial History of South Carolina Railroad* (Columbia: The State Company, 1930), pp. 1–221. The products of interior South Carolina such as cotton and rice were brought to the port of Charleston during the 1820s and 1830s by flat boats through the Santee Canal, which connected the Santee and Cooper Rivers and had been completed in 1800. The cost of such transportation including tolls, freight, and insurance was great. River travel was so hazardous that farmers preferred wagons. In 1830 the citizens of Charleston formed a company for the construction of a railroad that was to be run from Charleston to Summerville, to Branchville, to Blackville, finally ending in Hamburg on the Savannah River. The 120-mile route was opened on October 3, 1833, to passengers and for freight. The Sinklers would have traveled by cart or wagon from Belvidere on the Santee to the Branchville railroad station. The first engine was the *Best Friend,* while the *Barnwell* and the *Edisto* were put in operation when the line was completed. The amount of cotton shipped through Charleston as a result of the expanding line increased significantly, going from 186,638 bales of cotton in 1844 to 393,390 bales of cotton in 1859. Other freight shipped included barrels of flour, grain bushels, barrels of naval stores, and livestock.

52. Emily Wharton Sinkler to Mrs. Thomas I. Wharton, [September] 1842. The Charleston hurricane season lasts from August to the beginning of cold weather in October, and Emily with her September trips between Charleston and Philadelphia was risking serious weather for a small ship.

In one letter Emily is anticipating a trip home to Philadelphia, always by "schooner,"[53] and explaining why she is avoiding the hurricane season: "The anticipation of the visit is very much marred by the fear that I have fixed upon too early a time. But this has been such a stormy season and we have had two such experiences of September voyages, that I should dislike to try another one" (letter, August 8, 1850). Emily frequently traveled on the schooner *Emma.* The steamship advertised regularly in the Philadelphia newspaper *The Gazette:* "For Charleston, the fast sailing regular packet schooner Emma, J. Dickinson, master, now loading at Girard's Wharf, having a large part of her cargo engaged will sail as above. For balance of freight, or passage, having good accommodations, apply on board."[54]

On another occasion Emily was traveling from Woodford, which was near Bradford Springs in the Santee Hills, back to Belvidere and encountered high winds that made the ferry crossing perilous:

> On Monday morning at half past eleven we left and owing to the water in the Swamp [the Santee Swamp was between the Santee Hills and Belvidere] being very high we had to be ferried all through, and what is very creditable to relate in this age of magnetic Telegraphs and Atmospheric Rail Roads we accomplished the distance of three miles in three hours. Consequently it was very late when we got to the River and we had a good deal of difficulty in crossing. The wind rose very high when we were in the middle of the River and the boatmen could not put us at the landing. So we landed at a bank and had quite enough of the adventurous about the affair to satisfy my moderate aspirations for scenes. (letter, February 21, 1850)

Emily's closest friend and family member was Eliza, who, when she married Richard I. Manning, returned infrequently to The Eutaw. Emily describes a visit to Eliza:

---

53. *Charleston Daily Courier,* July 3, 1852, p. 3. Coastwise steamship service between the North and the South began in the 1840s and was regularly advertised thereafter. For example, there was regular service between Philadelphia and Savannah by the Steam Navigation Company's Line. The cost of cabin passage from Savannah or Charleston was twenty-five dollars, while steerage passage cost nine dollars. In 1853 the steamship advertised was the *State of Georgia,* weighing twelve hundred tons. It was to leave Savannah every Wednesday, and the "passengers by her enjoy the pleasure of river navigation one-sixth of the passage, remaining only two nights at sea."

54. *United States Gazette for the Country,* January 7, 1846, p. 2.

We set out on the 9th to go up to see Eliza. Crossed the River at Nelsons Ferry and as it was a long ferry went the whole way over the swamp in a flat. We got over very well and reached Aunt Richardsons at 2 o'clock. We stayed there that night and the next day went to Mrs. Mannings which is about 9 miles further on. We found Eliza and the baby both perfectly well; the little fellow is the image of Richard, quite plump and with a pretty little crop of thick short jet black hair. Eliza is just as satisfied with her two babies as possible and thinks it is all as it should be. She takes such things better than any one I ever heard of. (letter, March 18, 1847)

On the return trip a freshet, common to this swampy area, had caused the Santee to rise, and Emily experienced another one of those adventurous crossings: "Coming back we found the water extremely high, in fact a regular freshet, so we had a great time getting across the swamp and river and did not get over until 7 o'clock. The head boatman of the flat was a regular specimen of the tribe set forth by travellers. He talked incessantly and kept up the spirits of the rest wonderfully. We were nearly four hours crossing the swamp" (letter, March 18, 1847).

Travel from the low country to North Carolina and on into Virginia by personal horse-drawn carriage over potholed, mud-mired dirt roads was customary. On one occasion at Salt Sulphur Springs in Virginia in 1844 she had been on a carriage ride to see a magnificent view. Coming home the party was caught in a fierce mountain storm, and Emily's description of the scene is filled with enjoyment at the adventure:

When we were about a quarter of a mile from the carriage a regular mountain storm came up and we were forced to get in again with the addition of Eliza and then such a scene. All four curtained in and the carriage would bump first one side and then the other and the horses would rear and slip and Miss Hannah shrieked and Miss Sally shuddered. Miss Hannah would insist on peeping through the curtains. I told her not to. She would call out, that horse fell then, and now my side of the carriage is touching the ground. I could not help laughing but I was very glad to get home safe with only soreness from the jolt. (letter, August 27, 1844)

The distances must have seemed great when one was traveling on dirt roads in a buggy. Emily describes her itinerary on one trip to Virginia and comments that she has had enough of such travel:

If you would like to look out our route on the map I will tell you the principal towns we passed through going on and which we will go through going back. Going on Columbia, Winnsboro, Chester, York, S.C., Lincolnton N.C., Danville, Rocky Mount, Sweet Springs Va. Going back, Giles C.H. [Court House], Wythe C.H.,

Smyth C.H., Abingdon Va., Greenville Tennessee, Warm Springs N.C., Asheville, Flat Rock, N.C., Greenville S.C. I don't know which route we will take from Greenville for Charleston but I know one thing and that is I shall be very glad to get settled. Traveling in your own conveyance is pleasant enough for a few days but I have had quite enough of it. (letter, September 1, 1844)

The post was enormously important in low country South Carolina life because it kept far-flung plantations in touch with each other and the outside world. Emily relied on the post and anticipated each arrival eagerly. On one occasion a parcel had been lost and she is acutely disappointed: "Is it not too bad. I really am dreadfully disappointed and my jaundiced imagination pictures to itself the package as immensely large and containing long letters from every possible person. I hope the loss will be made up to me by new letters. I would not advise private opportunities however unless you are very sure of the person for indeed I think the mail is not so much to blame as you all seem to imagine" (letter, February 11, 1843).

Emily is very explicit in her directions to her family as how best to use the post to get letters to her from Philadelphia. The Sinklers used a factor to assure that their boxes and letters were received and properly forwarded. Emily describes the arrangement: "In the future when you have any packages or papers to send to me I wish you would direct them to the care of J. Chapman Huger and you will be sure of its reaching me directly. A Factor is expected to do every thing of that sort" (letter, November 15, 1845).

In a later letter Emily sends explicit instructions on how to get letters between Vances Ferry and Philadelphia the quickest: "There is a mail from Vances Ferry twice a week. A boy leaves The Eutaw every Monday and Thursday at 3 pm for the Post Office with letters and returns the same evening with letters that have come from Charleston. The letters we send down to the office leave Vances Ferry early on the mornings of Tuesday and Friday and arrive in Charleston in time to go on the same afternoon in the Wilmington boat. Consequently the letters we send to the PO on Monday ought to arrive in Philadelphia on Friday afternoon" (letter, February 16, 1848).

By 1856 improved, faster steamships were making the coastwise circuit between Charleston and Philadelphia, and Emily is excited about the quickness of the trip. "If the steamships succeed between Charleston and

Philadelphia it will be nothing of a trip. I am looking with some anxiety to see how the *Columbus* performs on her first trip" (letter, February 26, 1856).

Visiting in Charleston

Charleston[55] was forty miles away by rail, with an added ten-mile carriage ride from The Eutaw. It was the important shopping and commercial center for low country South Carolina. It was here that the ships for New York and Philadelphia arrived and debarked. Charleston was a wealthy port with substantial exports of naval supplies, cotton, corn, wheat, hides, rice, and much more. Emily loved Charleston, and her tone is always buoyant when she describes a visit there. She visited in Charleston for the week of the February horse races and for the annual Episcopal convention that was also held in February. Emily also stayed in Charleston or Philadelphia when she was in the last stages of her pregnancies, probably to avoid the difficulties of an unassisted childbirth.

Emily describes the setting in Charleston just after she has arrived on the schooner *Emma:* "It is very cheerful here, at dark always a good many gentlemen come in to see us and they bring round some coffee and a waiter full of enchanting little cakes made by the old black women. The bedroom looks so nice too when I go up there, the wood-fire is just lighted, the curtains of the bed drawn" (letter, [September] 1842).

Emily visited Charleston often, staying frequently with Charles's grandmother Mary Deas Broun,[56] an eighty-year-old lady, in a house which

---

55. Mrs. St. Julien Ravenel, *Charleston The Place and The People* (New York: Macmillan Company, 1912), pp. 464–500. "Never since the years immediately preceding the Revolution was Charleston so prosperous, so cheerful, so full of advance of every sort, as in those years between 1840 and 1860. . . . Her cotton and rice were carried in ships owned at home, her importations came direct from Europe. Her wharves were filled with vessels flying the American flag. The old Exchange, by this time called the Custom House, bristled with eager merchants and captains. . . . The theatre was on Meeting Street, near the site of the present Gibbes Art Gallery. It was large for those days and handsome. . . . There was always a good stock company, and stars came frequently. Fanny Ellsler danced there, Jenny Lind sang, and Rachel acted Adrienne Lecouvreur."

56. Mary Deas was born in 1762 in London and married Archibald Broun, a captain in the Revolu-

she describes as having four generations living in it. The house was at 39 Society Street. When that house was full, Emily stayed at Stewarts (a boardinghouse), The Charleston Hotel, or with her friends the James Simonses or the Henry Lesesnes.[57]

Emily's longest stay in Charleston was during the fall of 1847 when she and Charles booked rooms at Stewarts while they awaited the birth of their third child, Arabella (Ella). Emily comments that they "are very comfortably fixed here (Stewarts). We have good rooms and a private piazza in front of them and as we have our own servants it seems more like our own house than a boarding house" (letter, November 7, 1847). Emily describes the weather as delightful, warm like May and no frost yet so that people are "afraid to go to their plantations."

Emily obviously adored the fun and gaiety of Charleston. Her routine was one of teas, carriage rides, shopping on King Street, walking on the Battery, and going to dances and the races. She had many Charleston friends and mentions Hugers, Middletons, Izards, Frosts, Alstons, Ravenels, and Kinlochs.[58] She loved the fun of the city, which must have seemed a relief to the isolation of Belvidere and Upper Saint John's: "I am enjoying myself very much. A great many persons have called to see me, and my time is so much taken up that I can hardly spare a moment for writing" (letter, February 21, 1850).

The Sinklers went to Charleston every February for the races, which were a grand social occasion of dances, dinners, teas, and visits to the Washington racecourse. Emily describes the festive scene: "It is by far the best time to see Charleston to advantage as the Races being just over the

---

tionary War in 1780. Their daughter, Elizabeth Allen Broun, married William Sinkler, the beau pere, in 1810. Mary Deas Broun lived in Charleston and died at the age of ninety-five in 1857.

57. *Charleston Daily Courier,* February 2, 1853 p. 2. In the 1850s Charleston had a number of fine hotels of which the Charleston Hotel was the finest, costing $2.50 per day with dinner costing $1. Other hotels included Planters, American, Victoria, Carolina, Pavilion, Merchants, and Commercial. The rates of those hotels were $2, with dinner costing 75 cents.

58. Emily's Charleston friends included many family names still found in Charleston. Emily's closest Charleston female friends were Lizzie Middleton, Mary Lowndes, and the sisters Harriet and Elizabeth Huger, to whom she refers frequently.

gaieties of the worldly people were by no means subsided, and the concourse attracted by the convention had just begun. We took tea at Mrs. Frost's a family party to meet us, were invited to a ball at Mrs. Charles Alstons. The rest of the morning Anna Sinkler and I spent in shopping, I having a good many things to get for the house and servants. In the afternoon I took a drive on the Battery and paid several visits I owed from the last time I was in Charleston" (letter, February 18, 1851). On this occasion Emily, Charles, and the two children stayed with the Henry Lesesnes, and she seems to have had a wonderful time, concluding: "I never passed so pleasant a time before in Charleston, the only difficulty was that the time was too short" (letter, February 18, 1851).

On the same visit to Charleston Emily, Lizzie, and Wharton, accompanied by Edward, the beau pere's personal servant, went on a shopping spree on King Street:[59] "The next morning I sallied out accompanied by the two children and escorted by Edward. He walked behind in the Footman style, carrying the parcels and ringing the bells. Liz and Bud [Wharton] had been presented by their Grandfather with a gold piece each. However, the sight of the shops in King Street quite upset their little remains of prudence and they both relieved themselves of their money very quickly" (letter, February 18, 1851).

On another occasion Emily went to Charleston with Anna and William Henry Sinkler as the guest of the beau pere at the Charleston Hotel.[60]

---

59. *Charleston Daily Courier,* November 18, 1852, p. 3. King Street was the retail heart of Charleston in the nineteenth century. Emily might well have shopped at Miss Hanney's at 367 King Street, which in November of 1852 had "just received a beautiful stock of London and Paris goods, consisting of rich mantillas, cloaks of velvet, camel's hair, silks bonnets, corsets, etc." Or she might have gone to Mrs. Osborn, a "fashionable milliner" who advertised at her shop on 233 King Street a "large assortment of the most fashionable and approved styles of ladies' fall and winter bonnets, french flowers, feathers, etc." During the 1950s and 1960s King Street went into a major decline as suburban shopping malls came into vogue. However, beginning in the 1980s King Street has seen a wonderful retail and hotel revival, with many specialty shops, antique shops, and boutiques. And so today it is much as Emily would have known it with flower shops, boutiques, and dress shops.

60. The Charleston Hotel was on the east side of Meeting Street and has been demolished. In its place is a large, new neoclassical bank building at 200 Meeting Street. It was considered Charleston's finest hotel in the antebellum period.

Her letters are full of appreciation for the silk, ribbons, cuffs, and collars that the Whartons had sent so that Emily and Anna would look stylish in Charleston. Anna and Emily were close friends as well as in-laws, and Emily comments: "It will make it very pleasant for Anna to be there too and have her rooms adjoining. The beau pere takes down his carriage which will be very useful." Emily is concerned that she, too, look fetching for the Charleston scene: "I shall figure extensively in my new things" and have only "worn my new silk three times in the country, so it is quite fresh, as is also my hat in which I mean to put four violets and get strings to match" (letter, February 2, 1852).

Emily always reassures her family that Charleston is healthy, which was not easy given the ever-present dangers of malaria. "We are anticipating a great deal of pleasure from our trip to Charleston tomorrow. We heard from Dr. Frost that there is no epidemic there. There were some cases of measles of a mild kind. The reports we heard about Typhus Fever were very much exaggerated. The bills of mortality show the city to be perfectly healthy, not a single death from any fever or any catching disease."[61]

The children, Lizzie and Wharton, also seemed to enjoy the festivities of Charleston. Here Emily describes a military parade:[62] "The children are delighted with their trip. They are on the Battery,[63] constantly with Kitty, who I have brought down with me. Today there is to be a great parade of Savannah and Charleston companies and they have gone off in great glee to Harriet Ravenel's house to see it. Of course you remember Harriet Huger. I drank tea with her last evening in her beautiful new house on the Battery.

---

61. Emily Wharton Sinkler to Mary Wharton, February 2, 1852. Emily refers here to Dr. Henry Rutledge Frost (1795–1866).

62. *Charleston Daily Courier*, February 2, 1853, p. 3. Charleston had many military companies that paraded with great regularity. For example, on February 2, 1853, the 2d Brigade of Cavalry of Charleston were ordered to "parade at the Race Course, near Charleston on Tuesday 22nd, the line to be formed at 10 a.m."

63. The Battery is the sea wall that protects Charleston from the ocean. Its surface is of large flat granite stones. The wall is about five feet high and has always been a favorite place for afternoon promenades. In the eighteenth century there was no wall, and Charleston had many creeks and inlets.

I am sorry that our visit is so short; we will not be able to go to see the Russell Middletons" (letter, February 21, 1850).

Not only was Charleston in the 1850s prone to fever; it was also subject to devastating fires in which huge sections of the city were obliterated. Emily describes a fire in 1850 that she fears has taken one of her treasured boxes from the Whartons: "With the letter came a Charleston Newspaper dated the day after the letter which stated that there had been a very large fire in Charleston on Adgers Wharf, the Wharf of the *Osprey* [a steamer in the Charleston–Philadelphia coastwise circuit] and Mr. Simons' counting House. Altho Mr. Simons' name was not mentioned in the list of sufferers, yet it made me very uneasy lest the boxes should have been wet or injured in the confusion which always attends on a large fire" (letter, May 21, 1850).

On another occasion her friend Mary Lowndes's house has just burned down, and Emily describes her as having *"sang froid"* about the whole thing: "Mary Lowndes has just met with what would be considered a misfortune by most people. Her house which was large and convenient was burnt to the ground, a week before last and they lost nearly everything. Mary takes it with the utmost *sang froid* and says it is a most charming thing to live in a cottage of two rooms."[64]

Because the plantations were so susceptible to malaria for six months of the year, Emily and Charles were always looking for new retreats to escape yellow fever. Sullivan's Island was a popular summer resort because of its cool sea breezes. An article in the *Charleston Dailey Courier* for August 12, 1858, describes the settlement on Sullivan's Island called Moultrieville as having a Planter's Hotel, a Grand Palace "with magnificent piazzas looking out over the sea," Mrs. Fitzsimon's boardinghouse, and a fine old Episcopal church. In the spring of 1855 Emily and Charles rented a house on Sullivan's Island.[65] Emily apparently continued her tradition of wonder-

---

64. Emily Wharton Sinkler to Thomas I. Wharton, February 18, 1851. Mary Huger Lowndes was the daughter of Sabine Elliott Huger and Charles Tidyman Lowndes.

65. *Charleston Daily Courier,* July 3, 1852, p. 3. There was regularly advertised steamer service from Charleston to Sullivan's Island. "The new steamer Col. Myers, built expressly for this line, will

ful dinner parties. She describes the market with its fresh fish, crabs, and shrimp in detail:

> When I am going to have company to dinner, I get my marketing in Charleston, by means of Mrs. James Sinklers' old cook. Very nice fish can be bought at the Break water, nearly in front of our house. A remarkably nice fish called the whiting and Sheep's-Heads are the most caught. Crabs and shrimps in any quantity tho I have refrained from getting any. Every inch of ground near Charleston is now taken up with English and Northern Truck farmers. The white potatoes are really splendid and I am too provoked that there is no steamer running to Philadelphia for I want so much to send you a Barrel. (letter, May 30 [1855])

Visiting Family and Friends in the Country

It was the custom in the South during Emily's time to make extended visits in the low country to family and friends. Emily frequently returned to The Eutaw to stay several weeks with the beau pere and William Henry and Anna Sinkler. On one occasion she arrived for a splendid lancing, or jousting, tournament that was held at Pineville[66] eighteen miles from The Eutaw. Emily describes the festivities with delight:

> There were about two hundred ladies present, some in carriages, and from various parts of the country from Charleston and Columbia. Directly in front of the ladies' stand was the Ring, suspended from something looking it must be confessed very much like a Gallows. At long last the Knights were seen at full speed approaching, the trumpets sounding and as they drew near the Band struck up Yankee Doodle of all things for this anti-yankee state. At last they came before the stage, 30 in all, lances glittering and flags flying and after some manoeuvering the steeds were drawn up, lances lowered and the ladies saluted. Our friend Julius Porcher, "The Knight of Walworth," was selected he whose costume was the handsomest. His

---

commence her regular trips to the Island direct, tomorrow 20th as follows." The advertisement shows that there would be round-trip service six times a day. Sullivan's Island is the first barrier island north of Charleston. There were battlements there during the Revolutionary War, including Col. William Moultrie's palmetto log fort.

66. Pineville was another pineland summer retreat, like Eutawville. Very few of the old summer houses remain today. It is reached by going north of Moncks Corner to Saint Stephens and then west to Pineville.

dress was a full suit of armour which was certainly appropriate and looked extremely well on horseback.[67]

On another occasion Emily refers tongue-in-cheek to Julius Porcher: "Julius Porcher came here a few afternoons ago in his Philadelphia Phaeton which I believe you ordered for him at Watsons. It is really beautiful and very stylish. Julius is *in statu quo* and will probably remain there the rest of his life."[68]

Christmas was, of course, a family occasion, and Emily and Charles and their children returned each year to The Eutaw for the Christmas season. Emily talks about the custom of Charleston families spending Christmas in the country: "We have however not had so many as most of our neighbours, some have had 30 and some 40 in the house all the holidays. At the South all the members of the family spend their Christmas with the head of the family and no one stays in town who has a place to go to" (letter, January 1, 1845).

Christmas festivities included presents for all and a wonderful tree. Emily describes the excitement of the children over presents, the decoration of a wonderful tree, and the many preparations made in terms of food for so many guests. "This season of Christmas is here. In the first place, staying at Eutaw for nearly a week with the house there full of company, involves

---

67. Emily Wharton Sinkler to Thomas I. Wharton, April 25, 1851. Julius Porcher married Mary Fanning Wickham, and their daughter, Anne Wickham Porcher, married Emily and Charles's son Charlie Sinkler on December 5, 1883. Charlie and Anne had three children: Emily Wharton Sinkler, born October 23, 1884; Anne Wickham Sinkler, born November 4, 1886; and Caroline Sidney Sinkler, born November 7, 1895.

68. Emily Wharton Sinkler to Henry Wharton, April 3, 1855. Don H. Berkebile, *Carriage Terminology: An Historical Dictionary* (Washington, D.C.: Smithsonian Institution, 1978), p. 213. Julius Porcher lived from 1857 to his death in 1862 at Chickamauga at his beautiful plantation in Upper Saint John's Parish, St. Juliens, which is located just west of Eutawville. The house at St. Juliens has lovely black marble fireplaces which Julius brought back from his travels in Italy. The oak avenue is planted in the shape of a *J*. Emily refers to the fact that Julius had ordered a phaeton from Philadelphia. A phaeton was a four-wheeled carriage that is described as being lighter than other four-wheel carriages and more comfortable and safer than two-wheelers. Generally the body was built for the accommodation of two passengers. One of the main features of the phaeton was that, having no driving seat, the owner did the driving. It was considered a sporting vehicle. Generally the phaeton had a calash top.

a good deal of brushing up of the children's wardrobes, and then there is to be the grandest Christmas Tree ever known which is to be hung with wax lights and all manner of gilt things besides presents for the children. Then I have to help Anna [William Henry Sinkler's wife] at Eutaw in her preparations to provide for so many as will be in the house. Then the servants' Christmas. Not only do I give them all rice, sugar and coffee and Charles kills an ox for them but there is no end to the business of exchanging. They come to me with eggs and chickens for which they wish me to give them sugar, coffee, rice, wheat flour, tobacco, etc. etc. Of course I never refuse, and the consequence is I am at a loss to know what to do with all I have. I have now upwards of 100 chickens straggling about and an immense box of salt filled with eggs" (letter, December 22, 1851).

Emily's enthusiasm for staying at The Eutaw with the beau pere for Christmas was echoed by Lizzie, Emily's oldest daughter. In her *Memories of a South Carolina Plantation During the War* Lizzie describes the scene at Christmas at The Eutaw:

> At Eutaw my grandfather always expected his children and their families to spend Christmas and the whole week with him. In fact, that comprised every known person of the name of Sinkler. Nothing more unlike Christmas, according to Northern ideas, can be imagined. Early in the morning the negro fiddler would go through the house playing and singing, and the boys of the family with their black playmates were absorbed in making as much noise with firecrackers as possible. Then before breakfast there was the important ceremony of making eggnog in the pantry, in great bowls which were handed around with tall glasses.[69]

Lizzie, like her mother, was struck by the Sinkler custom of allowing the slaves a three-day dance on the piazza. As she says:

> Every day of Christmas week, in the afternoon, the negroes danced in the broad piazza until late at night, the orchestra consisting of two fiddlers, one man with bones and another had sticks with which he kept time on the floor, and sometimes singing. The last day that had been promised for holiday, they always began singing a sort of antiphonal chorus, "Do Mausser gi' me tomorrow, Yes, my nigger, tek to morrow." Then Grandpapa would come out and agree to that, which caused shouts

---

69. Coxe, *Memories of a South Carolina Plantation*, p. 88.

of thanks, and a servant would follow with a decanter of brandy on a silver tray and each of the older men would be given a dram.[70]

Traveling Home to Philadelphia

Philadelphia remained an important destination for Emily and her family. Her letters are filled with the excitement of going home, 150 Walnut Street,[71] for getting out of the low country and returning to a center of cultivation and civilization so familiar to her. Philadelphia was an important cultural as well as commercial city. Emily purchased much of her operatic music in Philadelphia from the music stores on Chestnut Street. There were regularly staged performances at the Walnut Street Theater and the Chestnut Street Theater. In January of 1846 there was singing by Marie McCartee as well as a Harlequin Humpback performance at the National Theater and Circus, and one could listen to Mr. Templeton singing his "Gems of Melody."[72] Emily may well have heard Jenny Lind at her final performance in Philadelphia in September of 1851.

Emily missed the excitement of the big city, the noise, bustle, cultural events, and access to good shopping. She speaks in this letter of having had too much of green leaves and roosters crowing:

> Our plans are thus. We all leave the Plantation on next Tuesday the 18th (the beau pere thinking it necessary to move a whole week before the rest of the neighbours) for the pineland where we will stay until the 27th when we will go to Charleston, sail on the 29th and be in New York I trust on the morning of the 1st of June and come on to Philadelphia by the afternoon line. I have had quite enough of green trees and roosters and am panting for brick walls and noise. I have been engaged in making preserves and jelly for next winter which I hope will turn out well. The strawberry seems so nice that I must bring on a jar with me. (letter, May 13, 1847)

---

70. Coxe, *Memories of a South Carolina Plantation*, p. 89.
71. The 100 block of Walnut Street is bordered on the eastern end by the Delaware River. Emily lived in close proximity to The City Tavern, Carpenter's Hall, and The American Philosophical Society, of which Thomas I. Wharton was a member, and down the street from Christ Church. The house is no longer standing, as the entire block was leveled to build a Sheraton Hotel.
72. *United States Gazette for the Country*, p. 3. The January 6, 1846, edition of the *Gazette* has advertisements for performances at both of the theaters mentioned above, as well as musical events at the Philadelphia Museum and at the Musical Fund Hall.

Portrait of Emily Wharton Sinkler

Emily did much of her shopping in Philadelphia, which was a center for imported European goods. Advertisements in the Philadelphia newspaper *The Gazette* proclaimed French flower wreaths for the head and French wall hangings, "white satin and gold and rich flowered papers"; Italian silks by "Mattioni, Veraias, and Rivas, and black Italian lustrings"; and "silk gloves," "taffeta ribbons," as well as "cut silk velvets" from Naples.[73] Not only did most of Emily's clothes come from Philadelphia, she also purchased her horse-drawn carriages there at Ogle and Watsons, a well-known coach maker. An advertisement in *The Gazette* describes the types of conveyances available from another coach maker, the Philadelphia Bazaar at 38 Dock Street: "well stocked with a new and fashionable assortment of light wagons, buggies, carryall wagons, barouches with standing and falling tops, charioters, close coaches. . . . The character of the work is so well known that it needs no recommendation. . . ."[74]

Philadelphia shopping expeditions were made for new furniture and for new curtain and upholstery material. Philadelphia was a center of fine cabinet making in the mid nineteenth century, and much of the furniture at Belvidere came from there. A sale close-out advertised in *The Gazette* gives some idea of the range of furniture manufactured in the city: "large and extensive sale of superior and well made cabinet furniture of the latest patterns and designs . . . , in the warerooms of M Bouvier & Co, 93 South Second Street above Walnut. Comprising in part, superior wardrobes; spring seat sofas, sofa tables made of rosewood and mahogany; dressing bureaus with oval and square glasses of the most modern styles. . . . The principal part of the above furniture has been taken in exchange from most of the best manufacturers in the city."[75]

While Charles often accompanied Emily home to Philadelphia, there seems to have been some suspicion that he did not enjoy the visits. As Emily says: "You know of course that I would infinitely prefer spending the summer in Philadelphia to any where else especially as in June it will

73. *United States Gazette for the Country*, January 15, 1846, p. 1.
74. *United States Gazette for the Country*, January 13, 1846, p. 4.
75. *United States Gazette for the Country*, March 9, 1846, p. 3.

37

be nine months since I have seen any of you, and if it is possible we will come some time in the summer. Mr. Sinkler says he begs leave to enter his protest against one thing which he says has been going on for now almost six years, and that is a sentence which is always put in your letters about his disliking Philadelphia. A charge which he solemnly denies" (letter, April 3, 1848).

Spring was a particularly nice time to be in Philadelphia, and Emily and Charles with their children rented a house in Germantown. By 1855 Emily's little clan had expanded to three—Lizzie, Wharton, and "little Charlie"—and there were too many to fit into the house at 150 Walnut Street: "As you cannot accommodate all at 150 Walnut St. it will be better for me and mine to stay at Frank's. We are getting very anxious about our Germantown House. What prospect is there for us now? Charles says he hopes you will be able to get one for $400 for the season, as this year it is very necessary for us to be prudent for cotton[76] is in a sad way which is very hard on those who have made 1/2 crops, all through this wretched war."[77]

Mothering

One of the central roles for women in the antebellum South Carolina low country was rearing and schooling children. By 1860 Emily and Charles's immediate family consisted of Lizzie, born in 1843; Wharton, born in 1845; Charlie, born in 1853; Mary, born in 1856; and the youngest, Caroline, born in 1860 at Belvidere. Another daughter, Ella, born in 1847, had died in 1848. Emily took an active role in teaching the children to read and to play the piano, while Charles taught them at an early age how to ride a horse.

Lizzie, the firstborn of Emily and Charles, was much adored. Emily, in

---

76. Woodman, *Slavery and the Southern Economy*, p. 40. A pound of ginned cotton was selling for thirteen cents in 1839, for five cents in 1845, and for eleven cents in 1853.
77. Emily Wharton Sinkler to Thomas I. Wharton, January 16, 1855. The war referred to here is the Crimean War. Germantown is a lovely residential area in Philadelphia just west of the old city where Emily grew up.

typical proud-parent fashion, brags of her accomplishments: "Lizzie is very well and improving very much. She is seventeen months old to day. She says a great many words and can point out the men, horses in a picture book very well. She will call me nothing but Emily or Emmy and her father Chaly. As for Papa or Mama she never thinks of saying either. It is certainly very disrespectful" (letter, December 7, 1844).

The Whartons sent an Irish maid, Catherine, to help Emily with Wharton, her second baby. "The baby is getting quite a distinctive character of his own. He is constantly trying all sorts of little artifices to get to suck his thumb which Catherine has waged war against" (letter, December 6, 1845). Emily, of course, had to hand-make clothes for all the children, and for a growing child this demanded time and energy: "I wish you could see little Wharton before he loses his fat. He has outgrown all his clothes much to my annoyance as I have to make new bodies to everything; shoes and stockings that Lizzie wore when she was 18 months old barely fit him now and he is only 4 months" (letter, January 1, 1846). The Whartons provided Emily with another maid, a Miss Scott from the North, and Emily seems to have been pleased with the help: "The children improve under Miss Scott, who is a very good conscientious girl. Lizzie makes steady progress with her music, and you would be surprised to see how composed she is on horseback" (letter, January 29, 1855).

Emily had both black and white nurses for the children, and it is interesting to hear what was expected of such help. "Eliza left her seamstress with me and I want her to do as much sewing as possible before we leave [for Philadelphia]. I wish I could bring her with me; she is such a genteel looking and handy girl. I suppose there will be no difficulty about my getting some one to suit me. I don't want a nurse as much as a servant; Bud [Wharton] is now 5 and Lizzie 7 so they need some one merely to wash and dress them and take them out occasionally. I want some one who can sew nicely and wash their clothes" (letter, August 8, 1850).

Ten years separated Lizzie from her brother Charlie, so it is not surprising that all eyes were focused on the new baby when he arrived in 1853. Emily was obviously delighted with her newest baby: "Charlie is droller than ever and you would be pleased to see how hearty he looks. I am afraid he has a very jovial turn. The first sound of music sets him dancing and curtseying" (letter, January 16, 1855). In another letter written on a rainy

Sunday afternoon when it was the family custom to read only religious matter, Emily describes a funny scene: "We had one of those country bugbears a rainy Sunday; no leaving the house for any one and only one religious paper. We were singing Hymns in the Library in the afternoon when a scene occurred which any one would have been amused with. You have heard of the Baby's great turn for dancing; well he entered, during a very solemn tune and at once began to dance, sometimes ducking down very low then turning round and round and all the time keeping time with one foot" (letter, January 29, 1855). Emily is obviously enjoying her little Charlie and in a letter four months later writes of him again: "Music and dancing are his specialties and I wish you could have seen a little incident a day or two ago. Charles went through the parlour to the Piazza to speak to some one and Charlie paddled after him full speed; just as he gained the door which was ajar Lizzie struck up a Polka on the piano. He was immediately arrested and began ducking down and dancing with all his body, keeping time with his head and feet and holding on to the door with one hand" (letter, April 3, 1855).

In February of 1856 Emily was back at Belvidere, enjoying country life but looking forward as always to the letters from home, and the boxes of books and goodies from Philadelphia. She had also had another baby, Mary Wharton Sinkler.[78] Emily was again enjoying a visit from her brother Henry, and in a letter she describes the evening dinner: "Last evening we wished particularly for you for we had a cheerful supper of fresh fried trout and bream" (letter, February 14 [1856]).

Missing Home—A City Girl in the South Carolina Low Country

Throughout Emily's letters there is a self-consciousness that what she is doing—living in the country, taking care of husband and children, going

---

78. Mary Wharton Sinkler was to marry Charles Stevens. Mary's children were Laura Anne Stevens Manning, who transcribed Emily's letters and placed them in the South Caroliniana Library, and Elizabeth Allen Stevens Martin.

to church, and visiting with a few friends—is boring and lackluster in comparison to what her Philadelphia family are doing. She has a difficult time hiding her envy at what she perceives to be the exciting events going on in her siblings' lives. Here she takes exception to her sister Mary calling her letters "circulars":

> Before going any further I want to know what you mean by calling my letters circulars. If you only knew how little I have to write about you would think it wonderful that I get through a letter at all. You who live in a city could have no trouble in writing but situated as you are when you know that the slightest thing about the family, the house and my friends and acquaintances affords me matter of speculation and wonder for a whole week, why you ought to write pages. What have I under the sun to write about. You are of course aware that nothing changes in the country but the seasons and one cannot be like Thomson for ever writing about them. Then if you did know the neighbours I would not be much better off for with the exception of our family we see the others but twice a year when on a formal visit. (letter, April 8, 1847)

Again in a later letter Emily anguishes over her "stupid" letters: "How you must gape over these stupid letters I write you, so different from yours. I wish I could change places with you for a while to show you that I have brains too. If you only knew the people here I could tell you plenty of amusing things, but as I am not Mme de Sevigne I cannot think of telling you anecdotes about people whose names you dont even know."[79] While it is obvious that her home at Belvidere was full of music, good food, and conviviality, it is also apparent that she yearned for the diversity and excitement of city life. It is also obvious that Emily kept abreast of the best literature of the time, from Dickens to the Brontë sisters. She read voraciously, from the *Bulletin* to the *Illustrated News* and any other paper that could be sent out from Philadelphia.

---

79. Emily Wharton Sinkler to Mary Wharton, November 7, 1847. *The Reader's Adviser,* volume 2 (New Providence: R. R. Bowker, 1994). Madame de Sevigne was Marie de Rabutin-Chantal, who lived in Paris from 1626 to 1696. The *Letters of Madame de Sevigne to Her Daughters and Her Friends* are full of anecdotes of seventeenth-century Paris.

Worshiping and Other Matters of Religion

Religion played an important and central role in the daily life of the Sinklers. There were morning prayers before breakfast each morning, and Sunday was strictly observed as the Sabbath: there was no work, and only religious publications could be read. There is much discussion in Emily's letters about religious topics, events, and politics. Emily's husband was a delegate to the annual Episcopal convention in Charleston, and he brought news of the doings of the Episcopal church back to Belvidere.

The Upper Saint John's Parish church, the Rocks, was seven miles from Belvidere, and it was the focal point for the Sinkler family's religious activities. Emily describes her activities with the ladies guild, and her concluding remarks indicate some frustration with the position of women in the low country:

> The ladies of the church have certainly done very well in 1852. In the way of improvement. They have added a large chancel, communion table, chairs, pulpit, and reading desk, chancel carpet and coverings for the pulpit, a complete set of new pews, a Melodeon, a church carpet and the church entirely painted inside. As I was one of the 9 or 10 ladies who did it all it came pretty heavy as you can imagine. I think it a great pity that the same set of ladies cannot act as vestry men for church matters would certainly prosper more. They have elected Charles warden and delegate, and the convention will be in May." (letter, February 8, 1853)

Easter celebrations were a special occasion for Emily and for the Rocks church. As she writes:

> Easter Sunday was the most splendid day I ever saw. Too cold for farmers with young crops just up, but not at all too much so for disinterested persons. We went to church having first made preparations to spend the night at Mrs. Converses', which is only a mile from the church but eleven miles nearer to Eutaw. I do wish that Mama could have seen the dressing of the church. It is a famous neighbourhood for fine gardens and every person brought a large bouquet of roses and these were placed in vases so that the effect was beautiful. Then the communion table, and pulpit were dressed with wreaths going all round." (letter, April 25, 1852)

Going to Sunday church was one of the big events of the week for all the Sinklers. Emily and Charles regularly attended church at the Rocks where Rev. William Dehon, the son of Bishop Dehon, was the minister.[80] They also attended Saint Philip's Church in Charleston where Rev. John Barnwell Campbell was first the assistant minister from 1840 to 1852 and then rector from 1852 to 1858.[81] Charles was a warden of the church at both the Rocks and Saint Philip's. Emily had great admiration for the preaching of both men.

In one of Emily's very first letters she describes Saint Philip's: "The handsomest church I was ever in. All the pews, altar and pulpit in short everything which is generally white with us is walnut there and the church is filled with splendidly carved pillars, very elaborately done. The ceiling is also beautiful." Emily goes on to describe the variations in the service from those she had been accustomed to in Philadelphia: "They have two things different from us. They have a clerk who repeats all the responses and gives out the Psalm and Hymn in the most stentorian voice. They also sit down while singing" (letter, [September] 1842).

Emily and Charles's life was very much centered around regular Sunday church, observance of the Sabbath, and church festivals such as Easter, Christmas, Good Friday, and Ash Wednesday. Emily attended Bible classes on a regular basis and reports to her family that while they are "very interesting, I assure you it requires a great deal of study to keep up. You can imagine how indefatigable the Porchers are in studying" (letter, January 12, 1852).

The Irish were suffering from famine in 1847, and Emily speaks of taking up a collection in the church for them: "We had a collection in our church last Sunday for the Irish but as most of the gentlemen had sent their contributions to town before it was not very large. The beau pere got up to forty dollars but stopped there" (letter, April 8, 1847).

Funerals were a time when families came together from all over the

---

80. Albert Sidney Thomas, *The Protestant Episcopal Church in South Carolina, 1820–1957* (Columbia, S.C.: R. L. Bryan Company, 1957). Rev. William Dehon (1817–1862) was the son of Sarah Russell and the Right Reverend Theodore Dehon, second Episcopal bishop of South Carolina. He was the rector of Saint Stephen's Parish, also Black Oak, Middle Saint John's, and The Rocks, in Upper Saint John's from 1842 to 1859. He was the rector of Saint Philip's, Charleston, from 1859 to 1862. He married in 1841 to his cousin Anne Manigault Middleton.
81. Thomas, *The Protestant Episcopal Church in South Carolina, 1820–1957.*

low country. Emily describes a funeral in Stateburg which she attended with friends, the Lesesnes, on a Good Friday: "On Good Friday we went to Church and afterwards went to what I had never seen before, a country funeral. One of the residents near Stateburg, Mr. Rutledge died and we were invited to the funeral and as Mr. Lesesne was anxious to be present we went. I was never more struck than the whole scene in that quiet churchyard which is in a beautiful situation, overlooking the distant river, the swamp beyond and the High Hills of Santee between."[82]

Religious tolerance has a long tradition in Charleston, which had congregations of every denomination, including Unitarians, Congregationalists, Huguenots, and one of the first reformed Jewish synagogues in the country. Emily was a staunch Episcopalian and may well not have appreciated the thriving religious freedom of her adopted city. She speaks with some condescension about an individual whom she describes as "the most bigoted Roman Catholic imaginable" (letter, December 16, 1851). In another letter she laughingly describes the Methodist views of a nurse her family have sent down to Charleston to take care of Emily during childbirth: "Well I asked Mrs. Campbell what church she belonged to. 'I attend the Methodists said she and I suppose I've joined them for Brother; [he] came to me and asked me why I never came to the Altar?' She has a strong objection to class and class leaders tho she acknowledges she can't do without Methodist preaching. So it was arranged that she should only be obliged to attend class once a month and then never tell her experiences and if you could only see her toss her head and say 'she tell her experiences, indeed' " (letter, December 10, 1847).

During the 1850s transcendentalism[83] swept the country, and it

---

82. Emily Wharton Sinkler to Thomas I. Wharton, April 25, 1851. Emily refers here to John Huger Rutledge (1809–1851), son of Ann Smith and Hugh Rutledge, buried in 1851 at Church of the Holy Cross, Stateburg, S.C. See *South Carolina Genealogies,* volume 2 (Spartanburg, S.C.: Reprint Company, 1983), p. 63.

83. Robert D. Richardson Jr., "Ralph Waldo Emerson," in *Dictionary of Literary Biography,* volume 59 (Detroit: Gale Research Company, 1987), p. 112. In New England Emerson and a group of followers began the transcendentalism movement, which rebelled against orthodoxy and dogma. "The group around Emerson usually called the Transcendentalists, were defined in one way by

reached the South where Emily describes it with the same condescension that tinged her remarks about Catholics and Methodists: "I am afraid from what they say the Russell Middletons are growing very transcendental. They have both got to undervalue regular church and prayer times to a dangerous degree. The idea seems to be with them that there is no occasion for family prayers, going to church etc. but that one must keep always in a state of prayer. Russell Middleton's great idea now is the love of God and that provided a person loves God everything else is unimportant, creed, profession etc" (letter, April 11, 1851).

Fighting Wars and Politics

Since Charles was a member of the United States Navy, the family was always concerned about the possibility of war. In a letter of 1846 Emily mentions the fact that enlisted men are looking for their orders, a "yellow" paper, in anticipation of being shipped out to the Mexican War.[84] While the Mexican War was apparently popular in the South, it was not so with the Sinkler family. Indeed, Chalres resigned from the United States Navy in 1847, probably because of his opposition to the Mexican War. "As to Mr. Sinkler's *Plouging the Main* he has been waiting orders since the first of last November but has heard nothing from the Department since, which has been the case with all his friends. I suppose Mr. Bancroft [George Bancroft, secretary of the U.S. Navy] has been waiting to see how the war question is to end. All the family in the mean time rushing to the mail bag twice a week to see if there is any yellow paper in it. I have been rather mortified to find that the Northerners are the ones who are so anxious for war. All here are opposed to it and lay all the blame on the North" (letter, February 28, 1846).

Emerson's 1838 Divinity School address, which offended orthodox Unitarians by locating religious authority in the religious nature of human beings rather than in the Bible or the person of Christ."
84. Ravenel, *Charleston, The Place and The People*, pp. 484–85. "The war was extremely popular with the people at large, who saw in it the opportunity for military distinction, and increase of territory for the South. The young men marched off gayly to win honour in the 'Palmetto Regiment,' under the command of General Scott, on almost every field from Vera Cruz to the City of Mexico."

The Mexican War was still going on in 1847, and all were eager for news from the front. Emily describes the scene: "How much I wished on Last Tuesday that there was a private Telegraph between Charleston and Philadelphia. I would have sent you the last Mexican News immediately for it arrived after the Wilmington boat left on Monday afternoon. I did not see the names of any I knew killed in the Pennsylvania regiment but several of our acquaintances here have been victims" (letter, October 24, 1847).

As tensions mounted between the North and the South, Emily was undoubtedly caught in a cross fire, with many questioning her loyalty to the South and South Carolina. She comments on her difficulty: "On Tuesday we paid a visit to the Rocks to some strangers staying there, two Miss Rogers from Rhode Island. One of them said to me 'of course you like the South much better than the North.' I was on the point of giving her a very haughty answer, when I saw two or three pairs of eyes fixed upon me, watching what I would say, so I swallowed my feelings and made a decent and pretty answer about comparisons, etc."[85]

Emily kept up with international news as well as she could. In one letter she speaks of the death of the czar: "We are all disappointed that the death of the Czar has produced no more peaceful result. I am afraid too that there is trouble brewing between England and France; in fact the plot seems to thicken all round."[86] On another occasion she is inquiring about photographs of the marriage of the emperor of Austria: "I have also received from him [Henry] several pamphlet periodicals which were very acceptable and I beg such favours may be kept up, not forgetting the *Brodeuse* from him and *Leslies' Fashion Monthly* from you. Also by the bye do send me any *Illustrated News* or any papers you may have containing

---

85. Emily Wharton Sinkler to Mary Wharton, March 8, 1852. The Rocks Plantation of which Emily speaks was about a six-mile buggy ride from Belvidere going in an easterly direction on Nelsons' Ferry Road. It was built by Capt. Peter Gaillard and burned to the ground in 1993.
86. Emily Wharton Sinkler to Henry Wharton, April 3, 1855. Bernard Grun, *The Timetables of History* (New York: Simon & Schuster, 1975). Emily refers here to Czar Nicholas I of Russia who died on March 2, 1855, and was succeeded by Alexander II.

accounts of the marriage of the Emperor of Austria. I have seen no accounts of it as yet."[87]

Confronting Slavery

The slave trade had been outlawed in 1808. In the North the antislavery movement was strong. The Whartons probably had freed blacks as servants in Philadelphia. The Sinklers, on the other hand, owned large cotton plantations: The Eutaw, Belvidere, Apsley, Wampee, and several more. There were large numbers of household slaves as well as field hands at each plantation.[88] When the beau pere died, he left 103 slaves among his three living sons. Many of the slaves were skilled craftsmen. The will names six "drivers" and eight "carpenters." Charles did not have an overseer and managed both Belvidere and Apsley plantations himself. The 1860 United States Census shows that Charles Sinkler owned 195 slaves.

Slaves planted, hoed, picked, and baled the cotton. They planted and harvested the wheat, rye, corn, and potatoes grown at Belvidere. They performed other plantation tasks, such as grooming horses, cultivating vegetable and flower gardens, and working in the house as personal servants. Work hours were typically long, from sunup to sundown, while

---

87. Emily Wharton Sinkler to Thomas I. Wharton, May 30, 1855. *Der Grosse Brockhaus,* volume 5 (Leipzig, 1930), p. 457. Kaiserin empress and queen, Elisabeth was born in Munich on December 24, 1837, and died in Geneva on September 10, 1898. She was the daughter of King Maxmillian Joseph of Bavaria. On April 24, 1854, she married her first cousin Emperor Franz Joseph I of Austria. She was an extraordinarily beautiful princess, interested in literature and the arts.

88. Woodman, *Slavery and the Southern Economy,* pp. 7, 13. Cultivation of cotton was well suited to slave labor as cultivation and picking kept a labor force busy most of the year. As cotton cultivation expanded in the antebellum South so did the institution of slavery. "Late in the winter the ground had to be prepared for the planting in early spring. Throughout the summer there was steady work thinning the plants and chopping out the grass. . . . Late in August the bolls began to burst, announcing the start of a picking season that continued well into the winter. As picking progressed, the cotton had to be ginned, weighed, pressed into bales, wrapped in bagging and then tied in preparation for its trip to market. . . . Cotton production allowed for the close supervision of slave labor. In both hoeing and picking, the slaves could be moved across the fields in gangs, and because cotton plants were low and did not hide the workers, a single man could supervise the labor of many." In 1790 there were 107,094 slaves in South Carolina, while by 1860 there were 402,406, comprising 52 percent of the state's population.

during cotton harvest slaves might work up to fourteen hours a day.[89] Slaves at Belvidere lived in slave quarters on "The Street," an area of cabins at some distance from the plantation house. Families, parents and their young and grown children, lived in a single cabin. The street culture was relatively autonomous from that of the Plantation House. There was a slave church built on a grassy knoll near a flowing spring.[90]

Emily's letters show that she had had very little exposure to Negroes in Philadelphia. She is surprised by their clothing, their singing, and their speech patterns. Emily refers to African Americans as blackeys, Negroes, or servants, but never slaves. Emily was all eyes, giving detailed accounts of the life around her, especially on the subject of slaves.

It was the custom in the South in the 1840s for black and white to attend the same church. In Emily's first letter home she comments on the fact that slaves attended Saint Philip's Church in Charleston along with white people:

> My good behaviour was very much tried in church and I am sure you will pity me when you know the cause. There are seats against the wall arranged for the black people. When I came into church they had not yet come but on looking round once it was almost too much for me. They were all very old people on our side. Such dressing. There was one old man in particular who seemed near 100. He was dressed in woolen pantaloons of a very grotesque cut with a flying Josey over it, a long scarf round his neck and on his head an immense white turban. All the women dressed with bonnets pitched exactly in the oddest way. They had prayer books and repeated the responses and sung, all rocking themselves to and fro. You can imagine what a sight it was for me to see 20 of them. (letter, [September] 1842)

The low country plantation customs for slaves were new to Emily. In an 1842 letter to her brother Frank she seems surprised by the unusual custom at The Eutaw of allowing the slaves to hold a three-day dance on the front piazza at Christmas (letter, November 28, 1842). She shortly

---

89. Peter Kolchin, *American Slavery, 1619–1877* (New York: Hill & Wang, 1993), p. 106.
90. Emily Sinkler Fishburne Whaley, personal unpublished memories. Mrs. Whaley is the great-granddaughter of Emily Wharton Sinkler and was frequently in residence at Belvidere from 1910 until its demise in 1940. She remembers over 120 Negro families living at Belvidere in the early twentieth century.

thereafter describes this custom in a letter to her father: "The Negroes would amuse you too much. The waiters are very much like Morris in some respects and talk very much in his style but the field servants are almost unintelligible. They are already making preparations for a three day dance at Christmas and are begging old clothes to make a figure in. They are allowed the use of the Piazza for three days" (letter, December 1, 1842). Emily continues the saga of the front piazza dance in another letter:

> On our return Eliza and I found on the steps a young black woman who after the accustomed salutation said she had brought a present. She had brought an apron full of eggs and wanted a calico dress in return to dance in at Christmas. A boy of 16 came in the afternoon for a cast off frock coat to dance in. William gave him a frock coat and I wish you could have seen him going up the avenue grinning at every step and turning around to look if any one was looking at him. They are making great preparations for their dance, though several are opposed to it on religious principles. They all call me Miss Emily but in speaking to me they say Missus. (letter, December 5, 1842)

Black fiddlers were renowned for their style and flair with music. Emily loved music and apparently enjoyed the black way with music. Here she comments on a black fiddler who lived at The Eutaw: "In the evening how you would all have laughed to have seen Allen and Huger [James Sinkler's children] dancing to the violin played by Orlando a blackey self taught. The door open and black heads of all sizes grinning in" (letter, December 10, 1842).

Issues of religious instruction as well as education of slaves were hot topics in the South in the 1840s. Slaves, especially field hands, were given no training or education. Most were unable to read or write as a result. Emily felt that black children were in need of both religious instruction and education. She apparently wanted to set up a school but thought better of it: "I wish I could do what Frank says with regard to the black children or frogs as he calls them but it is impossible. It is entirely forbidden by the laws of South Carolina and it would be very wrong for me to attempt to instruct them especially as Mr. Sinkler entirely disapproves of it" (letter, December 10, 1842). On another occasion Emily speaks of wanting to teach the Negroes: "I only wish I could teach the little blackeys. When Huger slept with me her little maid Serena slept also in the room on the floor. I taught her a prayer which I made her say every night and gave her some general ideas. I think there is a great deal more religion among them than you would think, for Rev. Dehon is coming very soon to give them instructions" (letter, February 11, 1843).

Separation of slave families was a well-documented, abhorrent fact of slave culture in the plantation-based, South Carolina low country.[91] In an 1845 letter Emily seems concerned about the fact that slave families were separated and were sent to different Sinkler plantations.[92] Her comments may indicate that she is trying to rationalize the custom to herself and explain it to her northern family: "When Mr. Sinkler bought Apsley all his servants were sent there and one day the mother of one of them came in my room. I told her I was very sorry Bull had to leave her but that he would have very little to do and should come and see her every Sunday. She said for her part she was very glad he was gone, that she had too many children already in her house, that his Maussa's was the right place for him, and I had better give him plenty to do. One named Mollo came to see me on Sunday and I made some consolatory remark to him about his wife, who is on this Plantation, when he pretty plainly told me that he thought her a good riddance, for she was continually fighting and scratching him. I feel very sorry for their perfect indifference to their situation" (letter, February 11, 1845).

Christmas was one of the principal holidays that the slaves celebrated, and Emily, delighted with the excitement of her first Christmas at The Eutaw, notes the big part the slaves played in the festivities: "Early on Christmas morning before break of day the Negroes began to arrive from

---

91. Kolchin, *American Slavery 1619–1877,* p. 101. Kolchin states that most southern slaves not only lived on modest holdings but also lived with a resident master. "In 1860 only 2.7 percent of Southern slave-holders owned 50 or more slaves, and only one-quarter of the slaves lived on such holdings." But see Theresa A. Singleton, *The Archaeology of Slavery and Plantation Life* (Orlando: Academic Press, 1985), pp. 220–22. This was certainly not the case for Upper Saint John's Parish or the Sinkler plantations, where the ratio of blacks to whites was more like 27:1. This exaggerated imbalance between whites and blacks meant that black field hands had less frequent contact with whites, picking up fewer of their customs and at the same time enjoying greater autonomy.

92. The Sinklers owned slaves at Belvidere, The Eutaw, and Apsley. Some idea of the number of slaves held can be gleaned from the will of the beau pere, William Sinkler, which shows that he owned 103 slaves. The United States Census for 1860 shows that Charles Sinkler owned 195 slaves.

the different plantations of Mr. Sinkler and I was soon awakened by a loud knocking at my door and then 'Merry Christmas Massa Charles may you have many years, and Merry Christmas Miss Emily, long life and prosperity to you.' One went to Brother James and said 'Merry Christmas Massa, may you have tousand years and have me to drive you horse all de time' " (letter, December 29, 1842).

Life on low country plantations was very much integrated in the sense that black and white formed an inseparable bond, with the blacks providing the labor and the whites totally dependent on the slave system. This extended to black and white children who were playmates from a young age. Emily's young children were surrounded by black playmates. Here she describes Lizzie in Charleston: "Lizzie is enchanted with the children. She walks up and down the piazza as stiff as possible with them and you would be too much amused to see the cortege that accompanies her in her wagon. Her four cousins pulling her and always at least four little blackeys holding on and all singing at the top of their voices, Lizzie joining in. She has the most unbounded admiration for them and they for her" (letter, October 7, 1844).

In a much later letter of 1855, Emily describes another exchange between Lizzie and a black child, Isaac: "One anecdote and I must conclude. You have I dare say heard of Isaac in our establishment, a coloured boy of 11, who does all sorts of odd things. On Sunday he showed Lizzie some candy which he had bought, whereupon she informed him that it was not right to buy things on Sunday. 'Oh but Miss Lizzie,' said he, 'you know I have not jined the church yet, so I can buy as much candy as I like on Sunday' " (letter, May 30, 1855).

It is interesting to discover that many of the sailors at the Navy Yard in Charleston were Negroes. Charles remained in the United States Navy until 1847 and did his tour of duty in the Navy Yard where there were many Negro sailors. Emily describes her concern for his safety: "Mr. Sinkler is at the Navy Yard to day. He is a great deal there and it is a very disagreeable place. He is the only official there and the sailors are all Negroes who are constantly in mutiny and he has the most unpleasant scenes; indeed I never feel perfectly easy; The Commodore is never there and there is but one white man besides himself ever at the Yard; almost every day he has to put some of them in irons, and he hardly gets home before some one comes running for him to come there" (letter, October 7, 1844).

Emily established a church for the Negroes at both The Eutaw and at Belvidere. She comments on the tradition of having black and white attend the same church: "A resolution [at the convention in Charleston] of Henry Lesesnes' also created a great deal of talk. It was to have a church or churches exclusively for the coloured population; now all are together" (letter, February 11, 1847).

Emily did not wait for such black churches to be established by the Episcopal church. She invited her minister, Rev. William Dehon, to hold services at both The Eutaw and at Belvidere. Here she describes one of the first of these events, taking special note of slave spirituals: "After church last Sunday Rev. Dehon came home with us to stay until the next day so as to have church for the servants in the afternoon. They behaved remarkably well, the women sitting on one side and the men on the other; there is something very wild in their tunes. It always makes me feel melancholy, but they persist in curtseying after every thing" (letter, December 7, 1844).

House servants were a special class of slaves, and being one was a position that was much coveted. Emily was aghast at the number of house servants at The Eutaw and occasionally in her letters appears to have thought it an inconvenience. Charles's sister Eliza married Richard Manning, and here Emily describes their return to The Eutaw for a visit: "Eliza arrived yesterday with her whole family on a visit. Mr. Manning and his brother and sister, the two babies, the two babies' two nurses, the last baby's nurses' baby with its nurse and the coloured baby's nurses' sister. What a cortege" (letter, April 8, 1847).

Emily and Charles carried slaves along with them on visits to Charleston to allow them to visit friends and family, as free travel by slaves was prohibited: "We set off tomorrow and in addition to several servants who we are going to treat to a trip to town to see relations, I have to take charge of Mrs. James Sinkler's eldest daughter."[93]

---

93. Emily Wharton Sinkler to Mary Wharton, February 2, 1852. *Charleston Daily Courier,* February 7, 1853, p. 4. One of the principal concerns of slave owners was runaway slaves. The *Charleston Daily*

Emily relied on her African American house servants Chloe and Rachel. She refers to them in her letters with praise for their excellent culinary preparations. Her receipt book, especially in the medical remedy section, indicates the extent to which Emily was the doctor for the entire Belvidere community, slave and white alike.

Telling Stories

Traditions and customs in the low country were perhaps not so unusual. It simply took an acute observer from the outside to note them with care. Emily had a keen eye for events and people around her. Her tales have a wry humor about them, with some gift for spotting the absurd. Here are a few of them. In the first she is referring to the surprise of all when Eliza Sinkler Manning produces a baby: "What do you think of her having a baby; we were very much surprised to hear of it for everything was done in the most Eve like manner possible" (letter, January 1, 1846).

Tom Kinloch was a friend of the family, and he brought his flute with him on visits to The Eutaw. Emily tells a tale of old Mrs. Kinloch and her weird ways: "Mrs. Kinloch came to see her [a friend] and took a great deal of notice of her little girls, told them that before they went she would send them a present. So the day before they were to go, her servant arrived with a silver waiter covered with a damask napkin. On opening it there was one baked potato in it" (letter, March 21, 1846). Another tale of Mr. Kinloch follows: "Poor old Mr. Kinloch is pretty old now but looks very miserable and neglected. Did you ever hear of the time he spanked an old lady about as fat as Miss Piggy from one end of King Street to the other?" (letter, March 21, 1846).

On another occasion she comments on dinner at Belvidere: "One of

---

Courier is full of advertisements seeking the return of runaway slaves, such as this: "Committed To the Charleston Work House, Lower Wards, a Negro fellow, who calls himself Joe Brown, and says he is free, but cannot produce any free papers. Said fellow has referred to several persons to establish his freedom all of whom deny any knowledge of him; therefore he is suspected of being a runaway. He is about 30 years of age rather slender built and 6 feet high. He has been employed on steamboats from this port. Any information concerning him either as a runaway or as a free man is respectfully solicited."

our neighbours sent us a piece of Kid which we had 'dressed' for dinner yesterday and I suppose Charles and the children felt quite patriarchal while eating. I confess notwithstanding the associations with Isaac and Jacob that I could not induce myself to eat it" (letter, May 30, 1850).

On yet another occasion she has seen something of a monstrosity: "Do you remember a very large child of hers when you were here? She has now the very largest baby I ever saw; when it was an hour old it weighted 17 pounds, and has been going on ever since growing in proportion" (letter, March 8, 1852).

Keeping Up with the Styles and Fashions

Women's fashions in the late 1840s and 1850s were of the Second Empire mode. Napoleon III and Empress Eugenie revived the French court, and the fashion-conscious empress set the style of gowns of silk accessorized with laces, ribbons, fringes, feathers, and flowers. Women of the time wore enormous voluminous long skirts, and the everyday dresses were accessorized with collars and cuffs.

Being fashionable at a time when most new clothes were made by a dressmaker required considerable talent and hard work. Emily had an obvious sense of style and a love of beautiful clothes, all of which were made for her by a seamstress in Philadelphia. Emily's dresses, hats, boots, collars, and gloves all came from Philadelphia. "My dresses are all beautiful and show a great deal of taste. The white is, I think, the prettiest dress I ever saw; I only have the chintz yet tried on, but as that fits me so perfectly I am sure the others will. Tell Clem [Emily's dressmaker] how much pleased I am with them" (letter, May 27, 1850).

Emily read *Leslie's Fashion Monthly* on a regular basis to keep up with northern styles. Emily was petite, loved blue, and favored silks, cambrics, and muslins. Her crayon portrait shows that she was as stylish as any of the painter Jean-Auguste-Dominique Ingres's subjects, and her classical looks evoke the world of European court painters.

Mary, her sister in Philadelphia, was her emissary for finding the latest patterns, purchasing cloth, and getting dresses made and shipped south. In an 1852 letter to Mary, Emily writes:

The patterns gave great satisfaction, so much so, that Charles was keen for my getting four dresses of the sort but I think that rather too much of one good thing, and am contented with getting one. Will you therefore get me 10 yards of the blue and Anna 10 yards of the brown? Please get me some patterns of whatever they have pretty at Levys in the way of Spring and Summer best dresses, and send them on in your next letter. You know the Spring begins here so soon that one wants thin dresses in April, and I have actually nothing to begin on. I enclose in this Ten dollars; after paying for my dress and Anna's there will be a remainder of 4.66. (letter, March 15, 1852)

Emily wore the usual accessories of the day, which she seemed to love, and most of which came to her from Philadelphia: "The parasol is perfectly to my taste. I never saw such a pretty one before. The ribbons are all choice; please let me know how to make them up, with ends or without, with hanging ends or straight ends. Both the collars are beautiful. The one you made particularly so, and tell me about the one lined with silk. It looks rather unfinished without any bow at the neck, and yet I have none which matches. Is your collar just the same? The cuffs you made are very neatly made as is also the collar. The gloves and boots are very nice and fit exactly" (letter, May 27, 1850).

Fashions in Charleston and the low country were mimicked after those of Europe, as shown in this mention of a French hat: "The cloak is very handsome and *comme il faut.* The ribbons very handsome. Anna has now a very nice outfit for her visit to Charleston. William bought her a very handsome French hat lately and several other things. He is so extravagant as a shopper however that she does not employ him often. She asked him to get her a twisted comb and he brought up one for which he paid twenty dollars; to be sure it was a very pretty tortoise shell" (letter, February 2, 1852).

With five children by 1860, Emily had quite a task of keeping them in clothes, let alone stylish clothes. However, the faithful Whartons sent the children wonderful clothes which supplemented the clothes that Emily made herself. Here Emily describes presents of clothes for all: "Thank you my dear Frank for the many pretty things you sent by Henry. To begin at the scarf and end at the Gaiters, every thing was appreciated. Bud and the belts are inseparable. Lizzie thinks of the muff as only a little girl can who has never had one before; the scarf was worn by Charles to the Convention [the Episcopal Convention in Charleston] and excited much admiration being the first ever worn here; my tooth pick case ornaments the *etagere* now, being reserved for choice dinner company. The baby sends her love to you and says she has lent the Gaiters to Bud until she is old enough to wear them" (letter, February 14, 1856).

Keeping House

Embroidery and handwork were an essential part of the life of women, as there were no ready-made sheets, towels, napkins, or tablecloths. Emily made and embroidered tablecloths and napkins.[94] She had to fashion remedies for cleaning linens and sheets, and in the receipt book she included instructions for taking rust from sheets. Her many ribbons had to be properly washed, and Emily thus had procedures for this in her receipt book. Emily was also accomplished at handwork, and thus it is not surprising to find a receipt for "Feather Stitch Knitting." Emily subscribed to the "valuable periodical," *The Brodeuse,* originally published in Paris in 1834, which undoubtedly provided her with embroidery patterns that were fashionable at the time (letter, January 29, 1855).

Emily had to fashion cleaning fluids at a time when one could not go to the store and buy brass and silver polish or shoe polish. It is not surprising that we find in her receipt book instructions for "Cheap, but Good Blacking" and "A Cheap Dye" as well as "Liquid for Cleaning Brass." Emily also made most of the soap used on the plantation, and we have her instructions for "Soap with Concentrated Lye" as well as "Potash Soap," "Cosmetic Soap," and "To Make Soap." Most of the soap used at Belvidere and The Eutaw was made on the premises. Emily's delight at real cosmetic soap sent from Philadelphia in one of the many "present boxes" shows how precious a commodity it was: "The soap has been universally admired; it is indeed beautiful" (letter, December 29, 1842).

At a time when there was no electricity, the low country night must

---

94. There is a wonderful old photograph of Emily's children, Lizzie, Mary, and Charlie's wife Anne all sewing on the front piazza at Belvidere. Each woman has handwork or embroidery in her lap. This author inherited beautiful face towels, with cross-stitching of the emblem *S* on each, and exquisite damask tablecloths with heavy embroidered monograms.

have seemed dark indeed. While there were oil and later gas lamps, there was also widespread use of candles. Emily had a receipt for "Lard Candles" and for an ingenious invention, which she got from *The Brodeuse,* for "Nightlights" that combined the use of horse chestnuts and oil. Undoubtedly, children and family went up to bed with candles and placed nightlights next to their beds.

But what was Emily to use in the place of such cleaning products as Windex or PineSol? She was not without ingenuity. In Emily's receipt book are instructions titled "To Clean Window Glasses" which required that one pulverize indigo to mix with vinegar wine.

Emily created her own formulas for shampoo and hair dye: "Hair Wash" included such ingredients as lac sulphur and sugar of lead, with instructions to wash the whole head twice a week. Another "Hair Wash" receipt called for castor oil mixed with alcohol. The receipt for hair dye called for a combination of lac sulphur, sugar lead, and rosewater.

Life in nineteenth-century, and especially in low country, South Carolina was beset with pests. Emily's remedy "To Drive Away Rats" required that one pound up potash and strew around the holes. The receipt "To Expel Mosquitoes" required one to burn camphor, and the one "For Bed Bugs" called for the application of kerosene oil. Given the death rate from malaria, it is apparent that the mosquito remedy did not work. Belvidere also had those unwanted creatures, ants. Emily's receipt "To Expel Ants" called for a sugared sponge loaded with ants to be dropped into boiling water. And to keep moths out of clothes stored over the summer, Emily's remedy was a typical low country strategy calling for the use of fresh branches from the cedar tree.

On one occasion Emily describes receiving over twenty-two letters in one mail delivery. Her correspondence was extensive and obviously required good ink, for she used a fine pen. She devised a formula for the receipt book for "Cheap and Excellent Ink" that used logwood and potash. She also had receipts for taking ink stains out of cloth and for making "Liquid Glues," which she used to great effect in pasting newspaper remedies into her receipt book.

Entertaining

Emily loved to entertain guests and did so frequently at Belvidere. The dining room had a large Early American cypress dining table that could seat twelve, and there was a big fireplace with easy chairs around it. The parlor likewise was comfortably arranged for entertaining family and guests. In her letters Emily often speaks of delightful dinner parties, and it is interesting to see how her menus used readily available plantation ingredients, such as turkey and eggs. In the following letter one senses Emily's amusement with low country chivalry, which she equates with bullying:

> On Saturday we received our neighbours the R.G.'s at dinner; this I mention as I wish Henry to know that his old bete noire the Turkey Gobbler was on that day sacrificed at the domestic altar. Of course he remembers the old Patriarch at Belvidere. Well he had become so insolent and chivalrous and bullying (the last two words by the bye are pretty much synonymous) attacking even Josey, that I resolved to have him cooped up and a week before the dinner he was killed and hung up. And what a monster; he had such a breast; he could have dined 13 people. Rachel made the dessert entirely and we had the best omelette soufflee we ever had, owing I suppose to our new oven.[95]

The receipt for "Celery Sauce" was a favorite of Emily's, and she mentions it several times in her letters. It was always an accompaniment to a turkey feast. In February of 1852 Emily had just had a large dinner party at Belvidere, and the menu was an interesting mix of low country ham, turkey, and duck, polished off with three desserts, again using local plums, eggs, cream, and sugar: "On Tuesday we had quite a large dinner party, mostly ladies, a very nice dinner: Vermicelli Soup, Boiled Turkey, Celery Sauce, Bouilli Ham; 2d course, Wild Ducks; Dessert, Omelette soufflee, Charlotte Polonaise, Plum Pudding, etc. etc." (letter, February 2, 1852).

Emily's particular forte was desserts, and most dinner parties ended with three desserts. She loved "Charlotte Russe" and omelettes, but most especially did she love ice cream. Her letters are full of yearnings for it, and the following shows her planning ahead for it: "How I wish you could all feel what a cold morning is the 16th of December. I assure you it is with difficulty I can hold the pen in my hand. I am however turning the

---

95. Emily Wharton Sinkler to Mary Wharton, February 21, 1850. Emily's neighbors, referred to above as the R. G.'s, were the Jno. G. Gaillards who lived at Ash Hill, a plantation in close proximity to Belvidere.

cold to the best account I can and have a man employed in collecting ice for future ice creams. I have already got a couple of barrels full and of quite thick ice too" (letter, December 16, 1851).

Emily entertained with great style, using some of her Philadelphia customs such as finger bowls with lemon and fan-shaped folded napkins, but very much employing a low country menu. She describes a fancy dinner party with gusto where the menu included venison and tongue as well as her usual three desserts:

> Since I wrote we have had another dinner party tho not large. Elizabeth Huger has been getting married and came up to pay Sister Margaret a bridal visit so we dined them. We had soup, boiled turkey and celery sauce, roasted haunch of venison and tongue for first courses; Charlotte Russe, epergne of custard and apple snow; I can see your incredulous look when you come to Charlotte Russe, but you may spare it for it was perfectly successful. I have Mrs. Hampton's receipt which she paid ten dollars for and every thing was right about it even to the ladies fingers around it. To be sure I had a very accomplished servant from The Eutaw to help me who has been accustomed to making them. You would have been amused I know at the style in which every thing was conducted, a roll at each plate, napkins folded fan shape, finger glasses each with a piece of lemon, etc.[96]

Cordials and bonbons were served as the finales to dinner parties. Emily made most of the cordials served at Belvidere from plums, blackberries, and cherries. She had many receipts using blackberries: three for wine and another for a cordial to be administered to the sick. Here she describes the custom of drinking cordials after dinner in the evening: "I know you would like very much some of the old fashioned customs they have. Large oak fires in every room. After dinner and supper when the cloth is removed they place in the middle of the table an old fashioned carved silver stand holding four bottles of cordial and place two decanters on each side and some glasses" (letter, December 1, 1842).

Emily had a sweet tooth, often commenting with delight on the bonbons from Henriades that the Whartons sent south. At Belvidere she made

---

96. Emily Wharton Sinkler to Mary Wharton, February 26 [1856]. Emily here refers to Mary Cantey Hampton of Columbia, S.C., who married Wade Hampton in 1801.

do with local ingredients for jellies and candies. However, the French influence is also felt. Here she describes her anticipation of using "Guimauve," a French word for marshmallow made from the mallow plant, to make candy:

> You would like Seaman Sinkler very much; I am quite delighted with him. He is so very attentive and kind. He has just been here to say that he has packed up a whole collection of books and sent them for me to the country. He has picked up a great many in Paris as he has lived there 3 years. He has sent on to The Eutaw among other books a perfect treasure. It is a receipt book of French receipts that he got in Paris teaching how to make all sorts of things. We were talking last night about French bonbons and this book is full of receipts how to make them. He knows how to do them himself and is now having made for me some Pate de Guimauve and Sirop de Guimauve which he is going to send to me with a root of Guimauve so as I can make it myself. If I can get any opportunity I will send some on to you. (letter, [September] 1842)

Living Off the Land

The Sinklers at both The Eutaw and at Belvidere lived off the land. They produced most of the staples including rice, Indian meal, wheat, oats, and rye. They made their own sorghum molasses. They had plenty of honey from bee-keeping. They had milk, cream, and butter but did not make cheese. They raised sweet potatoes but few white potatoes. They kept flocks of sheep and swine. They had herds of milk and beef cows. They hunted and frequently dined on haunch of venison and wild ducks. They fished and enjoyed shad in season and bream and trout from the Santee year-round. Their principal cash crop was cotton, as shown by this example: the Orangeburg District, which bordered Upper Saint John's, produced 16,315 ginned bales of cotton, each weighing four hundred pounds, according to the 1860 Agricultural Census.[97]

Emily's letters and receipt book attest to the fact that what one produced and gathered in by farming, hunting, and fishing was essential to

---

97. *Agriculture of The United States in 1860, The Eighth Census* (Washington, D.C.: Government Printing Office, 1864), pp. 128–29.

the welfare and survival of the family and the extended community of slaves. Any purchased provisions were shipped in from Charleston or Philadelphia. At Belvidere the staples were kept under lock and key in a tight storeroom that was located in the attic. The kitchen was an outbuilding, located at least twenty feet from a side entrance. During Emily's day it was equipped with an open fire over which iron kettles were hung. There was also a concave brick oven for making bread that was heated by wood from a hearth below.

The flocks of chickens, turkeys, and ducks at Belvidere were huge and were valued both for meat and as a source of eggs. Emily cooked chickens in "White Fricassees," in curry sauce, roasted, and in stews such as "Chicken Terrapin." The use of curry sauce shows a West Indian influence, while fricassee with its use of cream and eggs shows a French Huguenot influence. The receipt for "Chicken Terrapin" with its reference to turtles, and the turtle soup by the same name, was probably an African American concoction of Emily's cooks Chloe and Rachel.

Emily apparently enjoyed the task of feeding the ducks and chickens. Here is what she says about them in a letter:

> I wish you could have seen me in the afternoon. I went on the back steps as usual to feed the poultry about 200 in number. They have got very free with me and a rooster yesterday stood on my foot to eat the grains of corn off it. You would have laughed to see me going down to the creek followed by a black boy with a basket of corn and a whole set of waddling ducks who were straining every nerve to keep up with me. Being Sunday there were a large crowd of Negroes on the bridge to see me feed the ducks in the creek. The ducks dive in the most amusing way, quite to the bottom after corn. As soon as I am seen every black child exclaims at the top of its squeaking voice Huddy missus, howdy missus. (letter, November 28, 1842)

Emily regularly served wild ducks and partridges. She talks about the abundance of wild game in the Santee area: "We wished for you at dinner yesterday very much. There was a pair of wild ducks on table which were pronounced capital. Mr. Sinkler tells me to say they are infinitely superior to Canvass backs and red necks. They are duck and mallard I was told to say. There is an abundance of Partridges here; the yard is full of them but they are not allowed to be shot there. Snipe also abound" (letter, December 1, 1842).

Fish, like wild game, were bountiful in low country South Carolina, and both The Eutaw and Belvidere were near the Santee River, which had shad, bream, and trout. Emily cooked fish using a French receipt, "Poisson à la Crème," that had been sent to her from Philadelphia. Like so many of Emily's receipts, it used sweet cream and eggs to achieve a pudding consistency. Emily speaks of shad in one letter: "Give my love to him [Papa] and tell him I wish I could send him one of the fine shad that are very plentiful here now" (letter, February 11, 1843).

Emily made all of the plantation's preserves and jellies from apples, strawberries, blackberries, plums, quinces, pears, and figs, all of which would have been grown at Belvidere or gathered from the fields, wild. She remained on the plantation until late May and gathered early fruits as they came in: "I have been engaged in making preserves and jelly for next winter which I hope will turn out well. The strawberry seems so nice that I must bring on a jar with me" (letter, May 13, 1847).

Fresh vegetables were a treat of spring and summer, and so it is not surprising to find that Emily had many receipts for preserving tomatoes and making tomato ketchup. Her receipt "To Preserve Tomatoes" called for the use of stone jars and corks. One of the receipts for "Tomato Catsup" required cloves, allspice, pepper, cinnamon, and nutmeg all powdered together.

Emily talks of fresh spring vegetables like peas and asparagus. Her "Elizabeth's Split Pea Soup" used both fresh green peas as well as asparagus. "Are there any signs of Spring in Philadelphia? After having three weeks of warm weather, no fires and doors open there has come a sudden change which if it continues will blight every thing I am afraid. We are all shivering over the fire and having asparagus for dinner two things which seem to me rather dissonant" (letter, March 15, 1845). Emily had many receipts for pea soup, and she especially enjoyed peas as in her "To Make Winter Pea Soup." Here Emily talks about peas and strawberries: "From very wintry weather we have gone into summer the thermometer at 85 at 3 o'clock, children in summer clothes, the trees in full leaf, strawberries and peas expected in a week" (letter, April 8, 1847).

Because vegetables were seasonal, potatoes were a staple of life almost as prized as eggs on the plantation. Emily's use of Irish potatoes reflects her Philadelphia heritage, since potatoes were used there more regularly as a staple than such southern staples as corn and rice. Emily used potatoes in puddings, bread, and croquettes; as edgings for meat dishes; as a cheese substitute; and to make that all-important baking ingredient yeast. Her inventions with potatoes were some of the specialties of her receipt book. In her "Sweet Potato Pudding" she used sugar, while in her "Sweet Potato Pone" she used molasses. Both receipts called for butter and eggs. Emily's "Potato Croquettes" were a southern version of French fries, using mashed potatoes rolled in cornmeal that were then deep-fried.

Sweet potatoes were grown in abundance at Belvidere, and Emily shared this rich produce with her northern Wharton family. It is interesting to note in the following letter how Emily carefully tells her northern family how to cook hominy.[98] While Emily used Indian meal extensively in her receipt book, she had no receipts for cooking hominy. Emily describes a box, full of low country treasures, including rice, hominy, and light wood, that she has had shipped first by wagon to Charleston and then by sea to Philadelphia:

> The barrel contains sweet potatoes of two sorts, Yams and Spanish; the box has in it quite a mixture, four hams for you from le beau pere; by the bye he thought it was a great deal too few to send, a little bag of fresh hominy, one of rice and one of ground nuts and some light wood. Don't think you ever saw this latter. It is the dead part of the pine tree and is used here for lighting fires. I have sent you a little too; how nice it is it will light coal fires instead of charcoal. All of these are this years produce of the place and I intended also sending you some pecan nuts but they came after the box was packed. The potatoes I am afraid will not be good. They went down to Charleston in the waggon and must have been very much jolted; so as soon as they come to you you had better open them and take out the good ones. A very nice way to cook them is first parboil them and then slice and fry them; slice them about the thickness you do egg plants and lengthwise. The hominy must

---

98. Nicholas P. Hardeman, *Shucks, Shocks, and Hominy Blocks* (Baton Rouge: Louisiana State University Press, 1981), pp. 143–44. Hominy or grits, usually of white corn, "have been called the potatoes of the South, so heavily have they been relied upon for starch in that section. They are the 'sole food of the negroes' wrote an early traveler. . . . Grits were cooked as soup, porridge, or gruel, fried as cakes, or spooned on to the plate as vegetables."

be washed well in three waters and then boiled in enough water to cover it for fifteen or twenty minutes.[99]

Not only did Emily send sweet potatoes of two types north, but her family reciprocated and sent Irish potatoes south. Emily had just moved to Belvidere in 1848 when she wrote thus: "I believe I have never told you how delightful the potatoes have turned out. We have not yet taken any out of our barrel as we have some few left from our own growing and are keeping yours for great occasions but the beau pere has had his constantly and they are pronounced the finest ever seen in this latitude" (letter, January 17, 1848).

Rice culture and the low country were synonymous. The Sinklers had been rice farmers in Lower Saint John's Parish and undoubtedly brought many rice receipts with them when they moved to Upper Saint John's. Emily's receipt book showed that she quickly discovered local receipts for rice, from her friends and from her African American slaves. Emily used rice as an edging for meat dishes. She served sweet rice desserts such as "French Rice Pudding" and "Old Time Rice Pudding" that use boiled rice with cream, eggs, and sugar.[100] She used raw or boiled rice, often in combination with rice flour or wheat flour to make rice bread.[101] She made rice scones composed of flour and boiled rice. She had a cornbread receipt that combined raw rice and corn flour. Like hominy, made from cornmeal, rice was unfamiliar to Emily when she arrived in the South, and she comments on how her children are loving it: "Both he [Wharton] and Lizzie

---

99. Emily Wharton Sinkler to Thomas I. Wharton, November 15, 1845. Emily speaks here of "light wood," which is firewood made from the pine stump and is still used to light fires in the low country today. Because of the large number of fireplaces of different shapes, and the use of firewood for cooking, the task of cutting, sorting, and bringing in firewood was an important one delegated to a single slave and supervised carefully by Charles Sinkler.
100. Karen Hess, *The Carolina Rice Kitchen: The African Connection* (Columbia: University of South Carolina Press, 1992), p. 143. Karen Hess traces the sweet custard type puddings to both a French and an English provenance such as in "Rice Blanc Mange."
101. Hess, *The Carolina Rice Kitchen*, pp. 118–19. Hess attributes this combination of rice and wheat flour in making bread to the African American slave tradition. She notes that the loaf was typically baked in wood-fired ovens and was "cast" after being dusted with rice flour.

eat hominy and rice as heartily as if they never knew potatoes" (letter, December 17, 1846).

Products from cornmeal, which Emily called Indian meal, were new to Emily even though their heritage as polenta in Italian cooking goes back to the sixteenth century. However, she seems to have quickly learned local low country customs for making hot cornbread and for making soft, dinner spoon breads such as "Indian Cakes," "Baked Indian Pudding" and "Bannocks." All of these spoon-bread delicacies combined Indian meal with cream, egg yolks, and whipped egg whites that when baked formed a delicious, soft, spoon-bread pudding. Only with the "Baked Indian Pudding" did Emily sweeten with molasses. Cornbread had long been a staple of life in the South, and African American slaves generally cooked their cornbread without any shortening. One of Emily's receipts for cornbread was called "Virginia CornBread" and was made with eggs, butter, fresh milk, and cornmeal. The other receipt was from a neighbor and, interestingly, combined raw rice with milk, eggs, corn flour, and butter.[102]

Surprisingly, vermicelli and macaroni with their Italian provenance were particular favorites for Emily. Her macaroni dishes were made with milk, eggs, and cheese to form a delicious side dish. She made her own vermicelli following a receipt from Mary Randolph's *The Virginia Housewife*.[103]

Sugar was an essential ingredient for baking, for preserving, and for making desserts. Sugar was kept with other staples under lock and key in the storeroom at Belvidere. However, Emily's receipts also showed a liberal use of molasses. Sorghum was grown at Belvidere, and molasses was made by boiling it down into a thick syrup called sorghum molasses. Molasses would have been cheap in comparison to store-bought fine "loaf" white sugar. Emily used molasses to flavor plum puddings, for plum cake, in

102. Betty Fussell, *The Story of Corn* (New York: Alfred A. Knopf, 1991), pp. 233–38. Fussell traces cornmeal mush to Italian polenta and places its introduction in the low country South as a result of the African American slave trade. Cornmeal mush had been a staple in Africa from the sixteenth-century Portuguese trade. In the South, African Americans mixed cornmeal with meat skins, onions, and water and cooked it over a slow fire into a gruel.
103. Randolph, *The Virginia House-wife*, p. 100.

"Baked Indian Pudding," in "Soft Ginger Bread," in "Ginger Cake," and in "Sweet Potato Pone." Emily's desserts showed an inventive use of black-berries, plums, raisins, and apples, all mixed into a mincemeat or a plum pudding or cake with flour, eggs, and molasses. Her favorite desserts were the creams and custards in which she used Belvidere's wealth of eggs and sweet cream to great advantage. She also regularly served puddings made of bread, rice, potato, or cornmeal and topped these with sauces such as "Wine Sauce for Puddings," "Hard Sauce" from sugar, or "Pudding Sauce."

Emily's receipts were an interesting amalgam of traditions from Phila-delphia, Virginia, low country South Carolina, the French Huguenots, Af-rican American slaves, and the West Indies. Her receipts also showed that she was familiar with both Sarah Rutledge's and Mary Randolph's cook-books. Emily used invention and skill in melding these different traditions and sources, as one readily discovers when reading her letters and receipt book. Emily's receipt-writing style was a marvel. In three or four storylike lines she gave all the information one needs to complete the dish.

Coping with Death and Disease

Life in the low country of South Carolina was fraught with perils from disease, and Emily's letters and receipt book show that one could expect to suffer from scarlet fever, malaria, whooping cough, consumption, and many more. Emily lived before the time of antitoxins and vaccines for such diseases as tetanus, smallpox, and diphtheria. She describes epidemics of pneumonia, measles, and whooping cough that were not only killing but resulted in widespread quarantines. As she says: "We had made all our arrangements to leave here on Friday for a visit to Middle St. Johns but we have given up the plan now that we hear the measles have just broken out on all the plantations in that neighbourhood" (letter, March 8, 1852). And again a much-awaited visit from Eliza is delayed because of an epidemic: "I don't think Eliza will be able to come down this Spring for they seem to have one trouble on another. There was an epidemic on their place this winter, a sort of pneumonia or inflamation of the lungs, hardly one of the servants escaped; several died and the rest had severe illnesses" (letter, March 15, 1852).

The fear of disease and epidemics dictated family life. The Sinklers stayed at Belvidere and The Eutaw only after the first killing frost, sometimes as late as November. They left the plantation in late May before the mosquitoes arrived. In the interval they sojourned in pineland villages such as Eutawville, in the mountains at Flat Rock, North Carolina, or at Sullivan's Island off the coast of Charleston. Yellow fever and malaria were of particular concern because they were caused by mosquitoes which were thick in the low country before a killing frost. In Emily's day malaria was attributed to the bad air of the swamps and not to mosquitoes, a connection not made until 1880 by the French physician Charles Laveran. Emily told her parents, "You know it is perfectly healthy on the Plantation until the 20th of May and the family then go to the pineland until they arrange their plans for the Summer. One thing you may be sure of and that is the beau pere will not let me stay one minute later than it would be perfectly safe, for he is constantly uneasy for fear you and Mama will be uneasy" (letter, March 15, 1845).

Emily's medical remedies, as presented in her receipt book, are a reflection of medical practices in the first half of the nineteenth century. They are an indication of the constant presence of diseases such as tetanus and diphtheria, as well as epidemic diseases such as cholera, malaria, and yellow fever. Her remedies reflect a transition in medical practice that began to occur in the 1840s and 1850s with the discovery of methods to extract plant alkaloids in pure form.[104] Earlier medical regimes of the eighteenth century relied largely on powerful emetics such as calomel, tartar emetic, and ipecacuanha, and sedatives such as opium. Emily's pharmacy included these traditional remedies, as seen in her "Remedy for a Cough" and "For Cold with Fever in Children." But it also included remedies from an emerging medical regime based on plant alkaloids such as quinine and cinchonine from cinchona, and strychnine from *nux vomica*. Emily's medical remedies

104. Charles Singer and E. Ashworth Underwood, *A Short History of Medicine* (Oxford: Oxford University Press, 1962), pp. 671–87. An alkaloid "is a nitrogenous substance, usually of vegetable origin, which forms salts with acids. . . . Generally they occur in nature in combination with plant acids such as citric or tartaric acid. . . . The alkaloid group contains some of the most important drugs we possess, morphine, strychnine, cocaine, atropine, and quinine."

and her household formulas also show a familiarity with chemical halogens such as iodine and chlorine.[105]

In 1843, shortly after arriving at The Eutaw, one of Emily's young nephews, Johnny, died of pneumonia, and Emily reveals her grief at the death of one so young: "I carried the children over as the funeral service was to be read in the house and the body then carried to St. Stephens Parish where is the family burying ground. It was the saddest scene I ever witnessed; never did I see such agony as his father suffered. He took each child to the little body; none of them of course can understand it except William the eldest and he is heart broken; his little summer duck he calls him" (letter, January 18, 1843).

Yellow fever and malaria were terrors sufficient to drain the low country of white people in the summer, of course leaving the slaves, who appeared to have some immunity, to suffer the misery of swarms of mosquitoes. Emily describes a trip of several months duration, first to Salt Sulphur, then to Red Sulphur Springs, then to Greenville, Tennessee, and then to Warm Springs of North Carolina, and finally on September 16, 1844, arriving in Flat Rock, North Carolina:

> On the 16th of September I expect to be at Flat Rock where Mr. Sinkler will meet us. We expect to stay in that region and in Greenville S.C. until October. That is delightful climate in the mountains and the favourite resort for southerners who cannot come this far. The Commodore has given Mr. Sinkler a months leave and at the end of that time if there is any case of sickness in Charleston he will leave me near Columbia at Mrs. Mannings or Col. Hamptons until the frost, and thus far which is quite late you know they have not had a single case of fever and the average number of deaths has only been two whites and one black a week. (letter, August 27, 1844)

Emily was in her first year at The Eutaw when she came down with whooping cough which lasted over six weeks. She describes this racking

---

105. John S. Haller Jr., *American Medicine in Transition, 1840–1910* (Urbana: University of Illinois Press, 1981), p. 99. Haller notes that purging therapies lasted throughout the nineteenth century: "Armed with cups, lancet, leech and provided with calomel, tartar emetic, arsenic, . . . doctors proceeded to bleed, blister, puke, purge, and salivate patients until they either died from the combined disease and treatment or persevered long enough to recover from both."

disease, which was characterized by fits of coughing so severe that they produced vomiting:

> Before Christmas I got a little cough and cold which I thought nothing of until 4 weeks ago when I began to whoop.[106] Brother Seaman was up here about 2 weeks ago when it had nearly reached the height and said there was nothing to be done for it but time. He gave me a little bottle of paregoric,[107] squills,[108] nitre[109] etc. which I took one night but I did not sleep any the better. About a week ago he sent me from town [Charleston] another bottle a mixture of ether, belladonna[110] and opium,[111] a most horrid tasting thing but it did not do me any good. (letter, February 6, 1843)

There was a remedy for whooping cough in Emily's receipt book.

Consumption was prevalent in the nineteenth century, with no remedies that worked but much hope for a cure from taking the waters. Emily described the unpleasantness of being around these sick individuals in a letter to her brother Henry. She was staying at Red Sulphur Springs, ironically trying to avoid the fever in the low country: "The water is thought to be very good for pulmonary complaints and consequently there are the greatest quantity of consumptives in the different stages of the disease, all about. The table is very nice, delightful Charlotte Russes and ice cream with a regular bill of fare written out every day, but my opposite neighbour

---

106. *American Heritage Dictionary,* 2nd college ed., s.v. "whooping cough." Whooping cough is an infectious disease involving catarrh of the respiratory passages and characterized by spasms of coughing interspersed with deep, noisy inhalation.

107. *American Heritage Dictionary,* 2nd college ed., s.v. "paregoric." Paregoric is camphorated tincture of opium taken internally for the relief of diarrhea.

108. *American Heritage Dictionary,* 2nd college ed., s.v. "squills." Squills are the dried inner scales of the bulbs of the squill, used as rat poison and formerly as a cardiac stimulant, expectorant, and diuretic.

109. *American Heritage Dictionary,* 2nd college ed., s.v. "nitre." Nitre or niter is a white and gray mineral of potassium nitrate used in making gunpowder.

110. *American Heritage Dictionary,* 2nd college ed., s.v. "belladonna." Belladonna is an atropine powder derived from the leaves and roots of the belladonna and used to treat asthma, colic, and hyperacidity.

111. *American Heritage Dictionary,* 2nd college ed., s.v. "opium." Opium is an addictive drug prepared from the dried juice of unripe pods of the opium poppy, containing alkaloids such as morphine, narcotine, codeine, and papaverine and used as an anesthetic.

spoils all. Poor man he is evidently in the last stages of consumption and has an awful cough" (letter, September 1, 1844).

There were no remedies for consumption or other dire contagious diseases such as diphtheria and smallpox. Death was often unexpected and swift. Emily adored her husband's younger brother, Seaman Deas Sinkler, who was a doctor in Charleston. Her letters are full of references to him. One of Emily's most poignant letters describes Seaman's death from consumption:

> Our poor dear Seaman is gone; he died on Tuesday night at 11 o'clock after great suffering. For three days and nights before he died he was not able to lie down a minute but sat up with his head bent over on his breast suffering most acutely principally from suffocation. On Tuesday night at 9 his father [the beau pere] left him. Brother James and William also left him leaving Charles and Dr. Stoney an intimate friend of Seamans to sit up. At a little before 11 Dr. Stoney observed that his head had fallen back on the back of the chair and on feeling his pulse found it was going. The next day Brother James and Charles and William set out with the body in a carriage to take it to the family burying ground[112] in the most pouring rain you ever saw, cold as possible and very dark. I don't understand his disease. The physicians said it was galloping consumption but they gave him no remedies; he spit very little blood, hardly coughed and seemed nothing but a wasting away. (letter, January 21, 1847)

Emily's receipt book was filled with remedies for coughs, sore throat, toothaches, colds, and other such inconveniences of life. Many of these remedies called for simple solutions such as hot water and salt. Thus her "For Diarrhea" called for a teaspoon of salt dissolved in a pint of cold water

---

112. The original Sinkler burial ground was at Saint Stephens, a lovely Colonial church built in 1754. Earlier generations of Sinklers had lived on the lower Santee, and the Saint Stephens church served the whole lower Saint John's, Berkeley area. The church is twenty miles north of Moncks Corner. On Seaman Deas Sinkler's grave there is laudatory praise for his medical service to the people of Charleston, and expressions of grief at his unexpected and early death. His grave is immediately to the left as one ascends the steps from the street to the Saint Stephens churchyard. There is also a marker placed there by Anne Sinkler Fishburne, to the memory of those Sinklers buried elsewhere, namely her mother, Anne, and her father, Charles, both buried in Magnolia Cemetery in Charleston, and to Emily and Charles Sinkler, both buried at the Rocks, the remains of which are on a small island in Lake Marion.

and then bed rest, while "For Toothache" called for warm salt water to be held on the afflicted place. Indeed as her letters indicate, colds and discomforts were an everyday part of life. All of her medical receipts had directions for the amount to give a child.

Doctors had to make special visits to The Eutaw and Belvidere. Emily speaks in her letters of her doctors being Dr. Frost and Dr. Huger, both of whom practiced in Charleston. In her receipt book she attributed remedies to Dr. Porcher. Emily generally did not stay at Belvidere to have her babies. Ella and Mary were born in Charleston, and Lizzie and Wharton were born in Philadelphia. Only Caroline was born at Belvidere.

Emily stayed in Charleston at Stewarts for the entire fall of 1847 while she was pregnant with Ella. Emily's doctor for the birth of Ella was Dr. Francis Kinloch Huger, and she notes that he "came to see me a few days ago" (letter, November 14, 1847). Sometime between November 14 and December 10 of 1847 Ella was born in Charleston. In a letter of December 10 Emily says of the event: "You see I have again resumed the pen and you may look for my usual weekly lucubrations. I am happy to say we are all quite well. As for myself I feel as if I had taken a new lease of life. You can't think how kind every one has been since I have been sick in coming to see me and sending nice things; not one day has passed without something being sent to me. Mrs. Frost regularly every morning sends me breakfast; Lizzy Middleton comes every day and sits with me so I have been as comfortable as it was possible for me to be away from home" (letter, December 10, 1847). Emily goes on to describe the new baby: "I have often heard people talk of good babies but I never saw one before; she literally never cries during the whole 24 hours but once and that is when her head is washed. No cholic and she sleeps in bed" (letter, December 10, 1847). Ella was christened Arabella Wharton Sinkler on December 22 of 1847, probably at Saint Philip's. By January 3, 1848, Emily was back at The Eutaw among her family and friends.

Fighting the Civil War

There is apparently only one extant letter of Emily's from 1856 until the time of her death in 1875. The Charleston Historical Society has ten letters from Wharton Sinkler[113] to Emily, who was at Belvidere during the Civil War. These letters are full of love and appreciation for the boxes of provisions that Emily sent him. Emily and Charles also sent a servant, Mingo, to care for young Wharton during his various battle encampments in North Carolina and finally in Wilmington.

While we do not have Emily's description of life at Belvidere during the Civil War, we do have her daughter Lizzie's *Memories of a South Carolina Plantation during the War,* which was published in 1912. Lizzie's book was based on a diary she had kept during the war, and her account covers the entire five years of the war and is a moving story of its privations and terrors. Luckily, Belvidere, being twenty-five miles from the railroad and sixty miles from Charleston, saw no active involvement until the last winter and spring of the war. Sherman's troops marched through Bamberg, South Carolina, twenty-five miles to the northwest. Lizzie's account touches in several places on Charles's and Emily's actions and emotions during the war, and those are briefly excerpted here.

As the war wore on the little family at Belvidere felt increasingly isolated. Lizzie describes the lack of news and the long afternoons spent in reading with her mother. "There was a terrible dearth of news after this [Sherman's burning of Columbia], and we scarcely ever received a letter; and newspapers, of course, no longer existed. At this time when people were afraid to leave home, and we had no guests staying with us, my mother and I read through many volumes of French and English history, and she taught me German so successfully that we read with ease and pleasure most of Schiller's and Goethe's works."[114]

The end of slavery must have produced great uncertainty for Charles in terms of the future of farming at Belvidere. Indeed he spent 1866 in Philadelphia looking for work in the North, leaving Belvidere under the supervision of a caretaker from Ohio. However, friends and neighbors begged him to come home, and the whole family returned and set up farming and life again at Belvidere in 1867 with many of the emancipated

---

113. Sinkler Papers, The South Carolina Historical Society, Charleston, S.C.
114. Coxe, *Memories of a South Carolina Plantation,* p. 35.

slaves. Lizzie describes her father's actions on hearing of the Emancipation Proclamation: "After the fall of Charleston, my father called up the plantation and told them they had been proclaimed free by Lincoln, but they had better stay quietly in their comfortable homes. He also told them he intended to divide among them most of his provisions, which he did. This, of course, was considered quite quixotic by his neighbours."[115]

Because Charles had served in the United States Navy, he knew several Union colleagues stationed in the Charleston harbor. Lizzie describes the arrival of a gunboat sent up the Santee by Admiral Dahlgren to deliver a letter to Charles. The emissary was invited into the house, and "Papa said he was very glad to hear from his old friend and classmate, Dahlgren, but on reading his letter he said very stiffly to O'Kane: 'I am surprised to see that Dahlgren writes he supposes I am loyal to the United States. He knows very well that my loyalty belongs first to my State and only through my State to the government.' "[116]

Belvidere came under attack at the very end of the war by a Negro brigade with white officers. Lizzie describes the scene and the family's reaction:

> At last on this lovely spring day, after hours of anxiety, we looked out from the piazza and saw a number of negro soldiers running into the yard. Of course, the sight of negroes in uniform seemed to us an appalling thing, for nowadays it is difficult to imagine what a crime and horrible menace the arming of the negroes appeared to the South. Our own coloured servants came to the piazza and stood by us. The soldiers whooped and yelled for all the plantation to gather. They broke open the smokehouse, storerooms, and barns, and threw out to the negroes all the provisions and things they could find. At last several of them ran up the back steps and without even looking at us where we stood on the piazza went into the house and began throwing things about cursing and swearing, lashing long carriage whips about our heads and saying "Damed rebels" very often. Maumer [a loyal house servant] went with my mother after them into the house and tried to stop their injuring things, continually reproaching them for their misconduct. One of the negro soldiers snatched at my mother's watch chain and she took it off and put it into his

---

115. Coxe, *Memories of a South Carolina Plantation*, p. 36.
116. Coxe, *Memories of a South Carolina Plantation*, p. 39.

hands. He looked at the locket hanging on the chain and said; "Do you value the hair in this locket?" Yes, said she. He took his knife and picked the hair out and gave it to her. His conscience then seemed to stab him, and I am sure her beauty and lovely expression moved him, for he threw the whole thing, watch and chain, back into her hands and ran away as if from temptation.[117]

It is likely that communication by letter in the South Carolina low country during the Civil War was difficult, if not impossible. In her 1865 letter Emily suggests several possible means that the Whartons might get letters through to them at Belvidere, including using a flag of truce care of Mrs. Richard Manning at Manchester, South Carolina:

I have written you several times lately, being very anxious to set your minds at ease about us; but the opportunities were so uncertain that I will take advantage of a person going to a point near Charleston in an hour to write you a few lines. We are all well and getting on very comfortably. Things around us have assumed a quite different aspect from when we first wrote. So you must not feel any anxiety about us or take any more trouble for us. I should dearly love to hear from you all; it would be a great comfort but I fear there are inconveniences in the way of getting letters from Charleston.[118]

The Civil War was a time of emotional distress for individuals in both the North and South.[119] Sons and husbands were far away, and there was little ability to have firsthand, accurate information about their health and safety. Emily's family were all in Philadelphia, and her sentiments may well have been with the Union. However, many of her low country family were serving in the Confederate Army, including Wharton, who enlisted at the age of sixteen. Her anxiety for Wharton is palpable: "We have not heard from our dear boy since that letter of March 3, but a person who is a

---

117. Coxe, *Memories of a South Carolina Plantation,* pp. 44–45.

118. Emily Wharton Sinkler to Henry Wharton (brother), April 4, 1865, Sinkler Papers, The South Carolina Historical Society, Charleston, S.C.

119. E. B. Long and Barbara Long, *The Civil War Day by Day: An Almanac,* 1861–1865 (Garden City, N.Y., 1971). Civil War casualties were enormous. Total war-related deaths for those killed in action or those who died of wounds, or died of disease, or died in prison are estimated to be 665,850. Of these 405,850 were Union dead while 260,000 were Confederate dead. There were 501,000 nonmortally wounded individuals.

paroled prisoner told an intelligent servant of ours that he was captured 2 weeks ago at the same time he was, that he was unhurt, that he saw him after he was taken. This all seems straight but we must not give it much creed. But oh dear Hen this state of uncertainty we are in about him, the not being able to hear and yet knowing the constant danger he is in is most harrowing to my soul. Pray for him and for me."[120]

Emily was a person of courage and of love, and rather than bitterness and rancor she looked to a future where love would rule: "Ah when will all these sore and dreadful troubles be over. If we are not to see the end we still, thank God, have the blessed hope of a renewed Earth, whose only law will be that of Love. May each of us be partakers in its happiness."[121]

Epilogue

This 1865 letter is the last existing letter written by Emily Wharton Sinkler. Emily died tragically on February 10, 1875. She was only fifty-two years old. Her husband, Charles, survived her by nineteen years, dying on March 17, 1894. Both are buried in the Rocks graveyard, which is now isolated on a small island in the middle of Lake Marion. The Eutaw and Belvidere were both destroyed by the hydroelectric project that created Lake Marion and Lake Moultrie.

There was an eyewitness to the events of Emily's untimely death, Mrs. Henry (Kate) Wharton, the wife of Emily's brother Henry. Here is her account:

A service had been arranged for Ash-Wednesday morning. There seems to have been some doubt as to whether they would go. Charles said to me afterwards, "Emily was disappointed and said, 'it seems a pity for a Christian family not to keep such a day.' I said; 'Not a word more, you shall go.' " Emily came in and told me they were going to Church, and Lizzie would look after us. Mary went with them, all three in the buggy. Lizzie, Charlie and I established ourselves in the library. Polly took her

---

120. Emily Wharton Sinkler to Henry Wharton, April 4, 1865, Sinkler Papers, The South Carolina Historical Society, Charleston, S.C.

121. Emily Wharton Sinkler to Henry Wharton, April 4, 1865. Sinkler Papers, The South Carolina Historical Society.

books on the piazza. It was about one when Jeff came in. "Mass Charlie, de horse am coming up de road widout de buggy." When we got to the door the horse was standing still and we saw that the harness was broken. Charlie said he would ride back, while Lizzie was getting him some whiskey to take with him. I caught sight of Charles, rushing out of the wood, looking distraught. "is any one hurt" we called out. He answered, in a tone of anguish I can never forget, "Your Mother" then becoming calmer, "send for both doctors at once, Let Charlie follow with the carriage." With the help of the girls, I got the rooms ready, warmed the beds, heated water. It was not long before someone called "dey are coming." I went down the steps but Charles said "Kate you must not come you can do nothing. It is too cold for you here." As Emily was carried to her room. "I don't know whether she is living, she has neither moved or breathed." They brought her up on a mattress. I was able to help getting her into bed. Poor Mary had been terribly bruised and battered. When the doctor came he said "Charles, she is dead." He fell on the floor, Lizzie kneeling beside him. The doctor said death must have been instantaneous. The accident happened on the way home. They had enjoyed the service and sang the hymns "In Mercy Not in Wrath" and "Jesus Lover of My Soul." They stopped to warm themselves at Mr. Fullers. Probably the horse got tired to standing, as there was nothing to frighten him. After they turned in, the horse suddenly dashed off furiously. Charles felt Emily grasp his shoulder and heard her say, "Lord have mercy upon us" and almost with the prayer on her lips her soul took flight. As a moment later the crash came. They struck against a tree, tearing out the seat and part of the buggy and they were all thrown out. When Charles struggled to his feet, Emily and Mary were lying on their faces.

Kate Wharton tells of the funeral three days later: "A lovely day. It had been arranged to have the service at the house. I cut off some of her hair and Lizzie and I arranged a little cap of a soft, white, silk handkerchief to hide the bruises. She so full of love, tenderness and sympathy, lay in peaceful rest. The weeping servants stood round her, but no loud lamentations disturbed her quiet slumber. Charles' sister, Eliza Manning was here, the family from Eutaw, and some of the nearest neighbors. The piazza was full of Negroes. So she was taken away from the home of which she had been the light and joy."[122]

---

122. Mrs. Henry Wharton (Emily's sister-in-law), Extract from the Journal of Mrs. Henry Wharton, February 10, 1875, Belvidere. A copy of this letter is owned by this author.

Emily Wharton Sinkler, 1823–1875. The "light and joy" of Belvidere Plantation, Upper
St. John's Parish, South Carolina.

Eutaw Plantation, built in 1808 by the "beau-père," William Sinkler. Note the arched pi-azza foundations, whose brick was taken from the ruins of the house the British used as their center line in the Battle of Eutaw Springs.

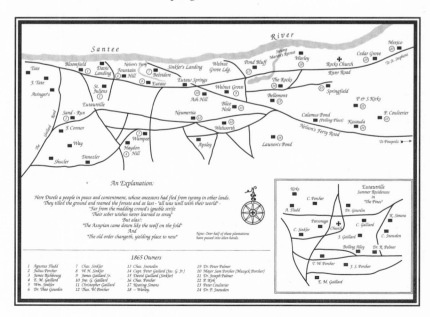

Plantations along the Santee River in Upper St. John's Parish, South Carolina, 1865.

Emily Wharton Sinkler as a young woman.

Pages 72–73 of Emily Wharton's Receipt Book, showing her fine penmanship.

Elizabeth Allen Sinkler, who married Col. Richard Irvine Manning in 1845, was the daughter of William Sinkler of The Eutaw. "Eliza" was Emily's best friend as well as her sister-in-law.

Belvidere Plantation, built by Margaret Cantey and James Sinkler in 1785, was the home of Emily and Charles Sinkler from 1848 to 1894 and the home of Charles St. George Sinkler and Anne Porcher Sinkler from 1894 to 1941.

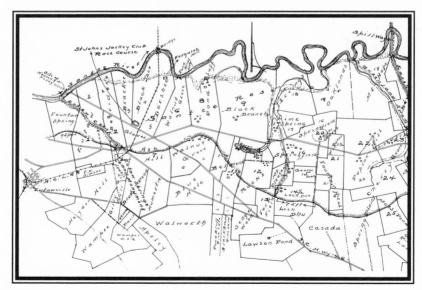

A surveyor's plat of Belvidere Plantation from 1942, at the time that it was flooded by the Santee Cooper Project.

The Belvidere piazza was covered with Cherokee roses.

Emily's daughter Mary Wharton Sinkler, who married Charles Stevens.

Emily's daughter-in-law Anne Wickham Porcher Sinkler, who married Charles St. George Sinkler. Anne was the "mistress" of Belvidere after Emily's death.

Emily's children Lizzie and Caroline swing on the piazza at Belvidere. Emily's daughter-in-law Anne Wickham Porcher Sinkler is in the middle.

Emily's children Charlie and Wharton (on left and right respectively) after a hunting party at Belvidere. Anne Wickham Porcher Sinkler is in the middle.

Epiphany Episcopal Church in Eutawville, South Carolina, built in 1849. Emily and Charles had a summer house in Eutawville and attended Epiphany.

Children of Belvidere slaves attending the wedding of Emily Wharton Sinkler to Nicholas Guy Roosevelt.

The Belvidere sideboard as it is today at the home of Anne Sinkler LeClercq, the author.

Belvidere in 1949, after it had been inundated by the Santee Cooper Project of 1941.

Maum Mary in the pepper patch at Belvidere while gathering ripe vegetables for dinner.

Three young workers in a sugar cane field at Belvidere. Cane molasses is used in many of Emily's receipts.

Feeding the chickens in the Belvidere barnyard.

The church for blacks at Belvidere was a center for social life.

Picking cotton was a labor-intensive activity. A gunny sack was slung over the shoulder to hold the cotton.

Emily Sinkler's gravestone.

A partial descendant list of Captain James Sinkler, down to the ninth generation.

Descendants of James Sinkler or Sinclair

James S. Sinclair — Jane

Captain Sinkler 1740 - 1800 — Margaret Cantey 1763 - 1821

Captain Sinkler

The b. Sinkler 1787 - 1852 — Elizabeth Broun 1785 - 1824

Margaret Sinkler

Henry Sinkler

James Sinkler

Charles Sinkler 1780 -

James Sinkler 1810 -

Dr. S. Sinkler 1816 - 1847

Charles Sinkler 1818 - 1894 — Emily Wharton 1823 - 1875

Elizabeth Sinkler 1821 -

William Sinkler 1819 -

Arabella Sinkler 1847 -

Wharton Sinkler 1845 - — Ella Brock

E. A. "Lizzie" 1843 -

Julia U. Sinkler 1872 -

Charles Sinkler 1874 -

John P. Sinkler 1875 -

Francis Sinkler 1877 -

Seaman Sinkler 1879 -

Emily Sinkler 1881 -

Wharton S. Jr. 1885 -

Ella B. Sinkler 1887 -

Charles Sinkler 1853 - — Anne Porcher 1860 -

Mary W. Sinkler 1857 -

Caroline Sinkler 1860 -

Sinkler, "Name" 1884 - 1970 — N. G. Roosevelt

A. Sinkler, "Nan" 1886 - 1981 — W. K. Fishburne 1879 -

Sinkler, "Carrie" 1895 - 1993

Fishburne 1911 - — Ben S. Whaley 1909 - 1987

Emily Whaley 1939 - — Grant Whipple 1929 -

Anne S. Whaley 1942 - — F. S. Le Clercq 1937 -

Martha Whaley 1945 - — Julian C. Adams

Fishburne - 1983 — Moultrie Ball

Anne M. Ball 1944 - — W. C. Helms III 1945 -

D. Balentine

D. Balentine 1968 -

Emily Balentine 1971 -

Frederic "Ted" 1963 -

C. Johnson 1969 -

Ben S. Le Clercq 1967 -

W. K. Le Clercq 1976 -

Sinkler Adams

Helen C. Adams

W. C. Helms IV 1971 -

Moultrie Helms 1975 -

Robert C. Helms 1981 -

Part II

Receipt Book

Emily Sinkler,
Charlestown, August 1st, 1855

❧ MEATS ❧

(Titles with the symbol • are for recipes and remedies from newsprint cutouts that were pasted into Emily's receipt book.)

White Fricassee[1]

Boil a pair of chickens not quite as much as you would for eating. Cut them up as about half. Put in a vessel lined with tin with a little salt, chopped parsley, 2 mace; cover over with cream and let it boil gently; just before you take up, roll a piece of butter the size of a walnut in flour and stir into the gravy.

Chicken Terrapin

Boil a chicken with the giblets until tender. Set aside until cold, then cut into pieces ½ inch square. Put into a stewpan with pepper, salt, 3 hard boiled eggs chopped fine, a teacup of the broth the fowl boiled in, a coffee cup of cream and piece of butter rolled in flour size of an egg. Set on the fire and simmer for 10 minutes. Then add a teacup of wine and serve.

Mrs. Putnam's Fricassee Chicken

Cut up the chicken; put in a saucepan with 1 pt water, 1 onion cut small, a little mace,[2] pepper, and salt. Boil 20 mins. Take out the chicken, strain gravy in a bowl; put in saucepan about 2 oz butter mixed with a large spoonful of flour. Put in the pieces of chicken, stir till hot, then add the gravy. Add a gill of cream and 2 eggs well beaten, and a little chopped parsley. Stir till it almost boils. [A gill is equal to 4 fl. oz.]

---

1. A white fricassee is generally made of chicken boiled down with gravy. Cream, eggs, and wine add to the flavor.
2. Emily used mace liberally. It comes from the red membrane that covers the nutmeg seed.

Boiled Turkey, Mrs. Markive

Take grated bread, butter, sweet herbs, pepper, salt and a little nutmeg, celery or oysters chopped according to taste. Mix up with yolk of egg. Stuff the turkey, flour it, tie in a cloth and boil an hour and ¼.

To Roast a Turkey or Chicken

After being well cleaned, let them lie in salt and water 1 hour; then dry and stuff with crumbs, butter, pepper and salt. Dredge with flour and baste several times with sauce of butter, while roasting by a quick fire.

To Currie Chicken

Cut up a pair of chickens and put in a pot with 1 pt water, 3 onions, and 2 teaspoons of salt. Let them stew ³/₄ of an hour; then put in 2 tablespoons of currie[3] dissolved in water; put in with it a piece of butter size of an egg and 2 tablespoonsful of flour rubbed together. Stew together a little longer. [A pint is equal to 16 fl. oz.]

Sweetbreads[4]

Put the sweetbreads in hot water for about 10 minutes; parboil ³/₄ of an hour, then pull off the sinews, skin etc. Dip in egg and bread crumbs and fry in butter a light brown; then put in a stew pan with a tumbler of

---

3. Sharon Tyler Herbst, *Food Lover's Companion* (New York: Barron's Educational Series, Inc., 1990), s.v. "Curry powder." Curry may be composed of up to twenty spices, herbs, and seeds, including cardamon, chilies, cinnamon, cloves, coriander, cumin, fennel seed, mace, nutmeg, red and black pepper, poppy and sesame seeds, saffron, tamarind, and turmeric.
4. Sweetbreads are the thymus glands of veal, young beef, lamb, and pork. Emily considered them a delicacy.

water, some more crumbs, parsley chopped fine and a little mace and salt. Stew gently for ½ an hour. [A tumbler is equal to 1 cup.]

Beef Scrapple[5]

Take a shin of beef, crack the bone, wash it clean, and take out the marrow; put the beef in a pot with six quarts of water; let it boil until the meat all leaves the bone; then take out the meat, chop it fine and replace it in the water in which it was boiled; season with pepper, salt and some sage rubbed fine; Stir in sufficient Indian meal to thicken it; let it boil about two hours and put it in pans and stand them in a cold place. In the morning cut it in thin slices and fry it until it is a nice crisp brown. This is a nice breakfast dish.

Veal Cutlets

Beat the steaks. Season on both sides with little salt and pepper. Beat 2 eggs light, and dip each cutlet in this, then into bread or biscuit crumbs till both sides are well covered, and fry dry. Boil the bone of veal and make a rich sauce with a piece of butter and flour size of an egg. Pour over cutlets ½ hour before serving.

Stewed Beef, Mrs. Scott

Take 6 lbs of the round of beef and put water enough in the pot to cover the beef barely; season with salt and pepper and boil until the meat is tender and then skim off the fat. Then put in onions, tomatoes, potatoes of both kinds, etc. When the vegetables are sufficiently cooked, thicken

---

5. Herbst, *Food Lover's Companion*, s.v. "scrapple." Scrapple is a Pennsylvania Dutch dish of scraps of cooked pork mixed with cornmeal, broth, and seasonings and cooked to a mush, then cooled, put into a pan, and often served for breakfast. Emily's receipt uses beef.

the gravy, and serve the meat in a large dish with the vegetables and gravy around it.

Bouilli[6] Beef, Jane Fowler

Take a rump, tie up, put in 2 skewers. Shake a handful of spices chopped up, having previously rubbed over with salt and pepper. Put in carrots; if large cut length wise. Put enough water in the pot to cover rump. It must only simmer, the pot often turned and the cover kept on tight. If it seems likely to burn add a little water as to make a gravy. When nearly done put a tea cup of flour into a frying pan to brown. Burn a little sugar, add a little water and mix with the flour with which to thicken the gravy. Sprinkle a couple of tablespoons of capers[7] in the gravy. Simmer from 8 to 9 hours. [A teacup equals ½ cup.]

Bouilli Beef, Mrs. Sitgreaves

Wash a rump and tie up. Put in a pot and cover with water. Add salt and onions, 5 carrots, 5 turnips, 2 bunches of pot herbs, 3 tablespoons of tomatoes. Must simmer 7 hours. As soon as it boils set it where it will simmer slowly. About ½ an hour before dinner take out the gravy, strain and skim off the fat. Thicken with flour. Give the gravy a boil up and add capers.

Pot Au Feu

Put in a saucepan six lbs of beef, bones included. Cut into two or three pieces; ¾ of a lb of mixed vegetables, such as onions, carrots, turnips, leeks,

---

6. *Bouilli* shares the same root with the French word *bouillon,* a broth made here from beef.

7. Herbst, *Food Lover's Companion,* s.v. "caper." Emily frequently added capers to her stews and sauces. They are the flower bud of a bush native to the Mediterranean whose sun-dried buds are packed in a vinegar brine. They have a pungent flavor.

white cabbage, and celery with the leaves on, all cut in good sized pieces; three small spoonfuls of salt, one of pepper and one of sugar; add eight pints of water, let it boil gently three hours; remove the fat; add crusts of roll or slices of bread, either previously toasted or plain, and serve.

Croquettes,[8] Mrs. Sitgreaves

Mince up very fine any kind of cold meat. For every 3 cups full put 1 oz boiled bread and milk. Add parsley, onions chopped very fine, lemon rind grated, 1 teaspoon made mustard and a piece butter size of a walnut. Shape with a jelly glass. Cover with yolks of egg and then with powdered cracker and fry.

Croquettes

Take 2 lbs veal, or chicken, parboil it, mince it as fine as possible; add two tablespoons butter, two three ounce eggs, with mace, pepper, salt and a little onion, parsley, and two or three tablespoons of rich cream. Mix all these ingredients together, form them in shapes, coat them with cracker crumbs, and fry them a light brown.

• Sweet Marjoram

Few know how to keep the flavor of sweet marjoram, the best of all herbs for broth and stuffing. It should be gathered in bud or bloom and tied in a tin kitchen, at a moderate distance from the fire; when dry, it should be rubbed, sifted, and corked up in a bottle.

---

8. Emily's use of minced meat such as veal or chicken in mounded ovals or rounds dipped into beaten egg and bread crumbs shows how she carefully made use of leftovers.

- *Stew Bones*

Bones from which roasting pieces have been cut may be bought in
market for trifle, and a very rich soup made of them, besides skimming the
fat for shortening. Bones from the rump are full of marrow, and will yield
a pint of good shortening, without impairing the richness of the soup. The
best pieces of beef for soup are the leg and shin; if boiled very long the
sinews add to the richness of the soup.

The shoulder of veal is the most economical for roasting or boiling,
two dinners may be made from it—the shoulder roasted, and the knuckle
cut off to be boiled with pork and greens or made into soup.

Fritodella

Take ½ lb stale bread; put in water to soak. Chop up ½ lb of any sort
of meat. Also potatoes and vegetables. If many of the latter are used more
meat is needed. Cut up a small onion fine and fry it for 3 minutes over a
hot fire with about an oz of butter in a stew pan. Then add the bread
which first squeeze in a coarse towel and remove the water, after which
put in meat and vegetables. Stir all together and mix in 2 eggs, gravy, 1
spoonful salt, ½ spoonful black pepper, little grated lemon peel and 1
spoonful sugar. After these are well mixed, pour into a bread dish and
when cold work into and make cakes. Roll with stale bread crumbs and
fry.

An Edging for Hashes

Boil 1 pt rice ½ an hour; season with a little butter and salt. Form the
rice round the dish about 3 or 4 inches high. Rub it once with yolk of an
egg and set in the oven to brown. When done turn the hash into the
middle of the dish. Potatoes mashed with butter, salt and milk formed the
same as the rice are even better.

English Mutton Sausages

Take cold roast mutton, cut in as large slices as possible; then bread
crumbs, sweet herbs, salt and pepper; net them with an egg; put a small

quantity into the center of each slice, roll each slice by itself and tie up as tight as you can. Lay them in hot melted butter and cook till brown and crisp.

Hashed Mutton

Rub a little flour and butter in a stew pan till brown. Then add as much butter as will make it the consistency of good cream. Put in some chopped onions; let them stew till tender. Cut 3 slices of mutton, put them in the sauce with some pepper and salt and a spoonful of ketchup and some chopped pickles. Make very hot and serve.

Poisson à la Crème

Five fish. First boil it, by putting it in cold water with a handful of salt. Second, pick meat off bones. Third, add a pint of cream and a piece of butter the size of an egg, and a tablespoonful of flour; boil the mixture five minutes, take it off the fire, and add the fish to it slowly; after all is in stir gently without mashing the fish. Season with salt and pepper to taste, turn all into an earthen pudding dish, grate a little cheese over it and bake for not longer than fifteen minutes in a quick oven; if cooked too long it is apt to spoil the cream. As soon as it is brown, it is cooked. If oven is not good use a hot shovel[9] to brown it. Lay slices of lemon over the top of dish. {This is on a letter dated December 18, 1870, from Philadelphia.}

Venison Pastry

Take the meat from a breast or shoulder of venison. Cut into pieces about 2 inches square. Crack the bones and put them with all the trimmings of the meat into a stew pan with pepper and salt and stew for 2

---

9. Emily's oven did not have a broiler. Thus she would use a hot paddle or shovel held over a dish to brown it.

hours. Strain this and put the meat you intend for the pie into this broth with 3 gills of Port wine, 2 onions cut in slices, a few spices and butter the size of an egg. Let the meat stew in this till half done. Then take out meat and put in a deep dish and pour over enough of the gravy to cover it, with a teaspoon of flour stirred in. Cover with pastry and ornament the top. Bake in a slow oven nearly two hours. Before it is sent to the table, add the juice of a lemon and $\frac{1}{2}$ gill of Port wine to the remainder of the gravy. Give it a boil up and pour it through a small opening in the crust. [A gill is equal to 4 fl. oz.]

Salted Fish[10]

A glass of vinegar put into the water you lay your fish in to soak will fetch out most of the salt.

Duck Stew

Take carcass and remnants of duck. Add 2 or 3 hard boiled eggs and 1 pint boiling water. Stew thoroughly. Add to this 1 tablespoon flour mixed with little cold water. Add salt, pepper, and capers.

Home Cured Hams

To 100 pounds of meat use 4 quarts of salt, 4 lbs brown sugar and 3 ounces of saltpeter well mixed. When meat is cold rub with $\frac{2}{3}$ of this mixture and pack meat away in a box or keg. Next day rub in the rest, then pack away again, reversing the pieces. Let remain 3 weeks, reversing pieces once a week. At the end of this time wash in warm water, wipe dry and smoke.

---

10. The Whartons sent Emily salted or pickled herring, and she preferred it as a breakfast or supper dish.

Ham Patties

Boil some potatoes. Mash them as if for the table omitting the salt. Chop very fine some pieces of cold ham. Stir it into the potato, make into patties and fry a rich brown. This is a nice breakfast dish.

❧ VEGETABLES ❧

Green Tomato Soy

Two gallons green tomatoes peeled and sliced; 5 tablespoons mustard. 3 gills mustard seed; 2½ tablespoons black pepper ground fine, 2 oz Allspice, 2 of cloves all pounded, 1 gill salt, 4 or 5 onions chopped fine, 2 qts brown sugar, 2½ qts vinegar. Boil all to the consistency of marmalade.

Pickled Mangoes[11]

Put them in salt and water for 3 days; make a slit through one half and take out the seeds. Put in the stuffing and tie round with a string that will not cut. For the stuffing 1 lb white mustard seed, ½ lb black, ¼ lb celery seed, 4 tablespoons pulverized black pepper, 2 oz pounded Allspice, 6 or 8 grated horseradish, and 4 or 5 onions chopped fine; green peppers, young tomatoes or cucumbers chopped fine may be added. Add 8 tablespoons brown sugar, and sweet oil enough to make it the consistency of thick mush. After they are stuffed and tied lay them in the jar and pour boiling vinegar upon them. Put in a little more brown sugar in the jar and 1 or 2 tablespoons of oil. Examine them often as the mangoes absorb the vinegar. Add more, and when too acid add more sugar and oil. Keep them by the kitchen fire for a week or so.

---

11. These may not be true mangoes, but bell peppers. In Pennsylvania bell peppers were often called mangoes. The techniques in this receipt, such as slit one in half and take out the seeds, seem to indicate this is a green pepper. I would like to thank Karen Hess for this information.

Chili Sauce

Nine large ripe tomatoes, 2 onions, 1 green pepper, ½ cup sugar, 1 cup vinegar, 1 tablespoon salt, 1 teaspoon cinnamon, 1 teaspoon Allspice, 1 teaspoon mustard. Chop onions and green pepper, add tomatoes cut in pieces and sugar. Boil until thick. Add vinegar, salt and spices, and boil 5 minutes. Seal in glass jars and cover.

• *Vinegar*

Take one quart of blackberries and three quarts of water and two spoonsful of sugar or molasses, put in a demijohn and set it in the sun for about two weeks, and you will have excellent vinegar.

Salad Dressing, Mrs. Randolph

Boil two fresh eggs 10 minutes; put them in water to cool, then put the yolks in a soup plate; pour on them a tablespoon of cold water; rub them with a wooden spoon until well dissolved; then add 4 tablespoons of oil. When well mixed, put in 1 teaspoonful of salt and one of made mustard; when all these are united and quite smooth, stir in two tablespoons of vinegar; put it over the salad which must be cut up.

• *Potatoes*[12]

At this season of the year potatoes become soft, and are not so readily cooked as when hard. A Vermont woman publishes the following receipt,

---

12. Herbst, *Food Lover's Companion*, s.v. "potato." In her letters and receipts Emily speaks of having two types of white potatoes. The tuber is native to South America and was transported to Ireland by Sir Walter Raleigh. There are four basic types of potatoes: russet, long white, round white, and round red. The sweet potato is of a different origin, the morning-glory family, and is also native to tropical America. Emily used both white potatoes and sweet potatoes in her many potato receipts.

which we recommend for trial. The potatoes are pared and put to soak in cold water from four to six hours; then dropped into water which is already boiling, an essential point; and a little salt added to the water improves them. Take them from the fire the moment they are done; pour off all the water, and let them stand uncovered in the kettle over the fire till the water evaporates from the surface, and they are ready for the table. The result will astonish those who try it for the first time, and they will never return to the old method of boiling them with the skins on.

Potatoes a la Lyonnaise

When freshly boiled or cold potatoes sliced thru. Put 3 ozs butter in a frying pan. Slice 3 onions in it, fry a light brown. Then put in the potatoes and stir about till of a nice yellow. Add a large spoonful of chopped parsley, salt, pepper and the juice of a lemon. Toss while over the fire so that they may be thoroughly mixed.

Maitre d'Hotel Potatoes

Boil the potatoes, cut in moderately thick slices. Then stew a few minutes in a sauce of butter melted in milk, and brush with a little minced parsley, pepper, salt and juice of a lemon.

Mashed Potatoes, Mrs. Lamae

Pare and try to have all of the same size so that they may be equally boiled; put in boiling water and boil 15 minutes, not too fast lest they break; let them stay in water till ready to mash them; pour off the water and pound in the same vessel with a masher till smooth. Add a piece of butter size of egg for a large dish full or about 13 good sized potatoes; then take a wooden spoon and beat as you would eggs; add a small tea cup of milk; put the vessel on the fire and continue beating until light and white.

To Boil Potatoes, Mrs F. R. Wharton

Slit them slightly, put in a pot, cover with cold water, boil hard for 20 minutes. Take out and squeeze in a warm dry towel. The pot to be uncovered.

To Boil Potatoes

Pare and soak 1 hour in cold water before boiling; then boil the usual time; when done squeeze through a dry towel till all the moisture is out.

Potato Croquettes

Boil a dozen nice potatoes until soft. Mash with milk, butter and seasoning, also a little chopped parsley. Add a soupcon of onion. Let cool for an hour or two, then shape and roll in grated bread crumbs; drop in the yolk of an egg, then back into the bread crumbs. Fry in hot grease and place in pan. Keep warm in an oven.

Corn Fritters, Mrs. Duane

Take 12 small ears of corn, cut the grains down the centre and scrape all the grains and milk off the cob. Add about 2 tablespoons of flour; beat 2 eggs, add pepper and salt to your taste and mix the whole together. Put a tablespoonful at a time in a frying pan with hot butter; when brown turn and serve hot. If the corn is large it will require 3 eggs, if milky a little extra flour should be added. Should be rather thicker than pan cake batter. Will cook in 5 minutes.

Satira's Corn Pie

Six ears corn, salt to taste, 3 eggs, 1 tablespoon butter, dessert spoon flour. Grate corn, add eggs which have been well beaten, then butter, salt, flour, and enough milk to make really soft. Bake in moderate oven.

Mushrooms, J. Biddle

One qt makes a good sized dish; carefully peel off the thin skin; sprinkle with ½ teaspoon salt, and let them stand for several hours in a covered dish. If for breakfast prepare night before, then add pepper, a piece of butter and let them simmer for 20 minutes; give a boil up and serve.

Scalloped Tomatoes

Peel full ripe tomatoes; slice in thin slices and put a layer in bottom of dish, season with salt, pepper and sugar. Cover with bread crumbs and small pieces of butter. Add more layers of the same until dish is full. Let the top layer be bread crumbs and bake a nice brown.

To Preserve Tomatoes

Prepare as for cooking; boil 1 hour; put in stone jars, then cork and boil the jars 2 hours; take out and seal air tight. Should be seasoned and cooked for ½ an hour when opened.

Mr. R. Simons Recipe for Preserving Tomatoes

The tomatoes must be freshly picked. Peel them with a knife without scalding, cut up and fill dry wine bottles. Put in a large pot with sufficient cold water; let the water boil and the bottles till the steam has ceased rising. Cork or cement while the bottles are in the water. After some days if a white substance rises to the top it is a sign that they are good; if not better take out and boil over.

Tomato Catsup

Wash your Tomatoes and slice them up; put a layer of tomatoes and a layer of salt; let them remain all night, then pour off the water extracted by the salt. Put the tomatoes into a pot perfectly free from grease and stew until done. Then strain through a sieve. Season with vinegar, Allspice, ginger, salt and powdered red pepper to your taste; return to the pot and stew that down to about half. If not thick enough add a piece of green ginger.[13] Seal the bottles if not required for immediate use. I send a bottle of Catsup for you to take on to Lizzie with my love, Yours ERS. [addressed on the outside to Emily Sinkler]

Tomato Catsup

Squeeze the tomatoes through a sieve. To 6 quarts add 3 quarts vinegar. Set over a slow fire to boil. When it begins to thicken add 1/2 oz each of cloves, Allspice and pepper, 1/4 oz of cinnamon and 2 nutmegs all finely powdered. Boil till like thin mush. Then add 4 tablespoons salt. When cold bottle and seal. Boil in a porcelain kettle or remove from a brass or tin before adding salt.

Celery Sauce

Wash and pare a large bunch very clean; Cut into little bits and boil swiftly till tender; add 1/2 pt cream, some mace, nutmeg, and small piece of butter rolled in flour, then boil gently and serve.

Essence of Celery

Steep an ounce of celery seed in half a pint of brandy or vinegar. A few drops of this will give a fine flavor to soups and sauce for fowls.

Cold Sauce, Balbirnie Sauce

A small shallot chopped as fine as possible; one spoonful of mustard, one tablespoon of oil. Mix thoroughly and add a little salt, one tablespoon of vinegar, and two of ketchup. This is excellent.

---

13. Herbst, *Food Lover's Companion,* s.v. "ginger." Ginger root comes from Jamaica and has a peppery, slightly sweet flavor. It is interesting to note that ginger is used here to thicken catsup.

- *Stewed Spinach*

Pick the spinach very clean, and wash it through two or three waters; then drain it and put it into a saucepan, with only the water that remains about it after the washing; add a very little salt and pepper, and let it stew for twenty minutes, or till it is quite tender, turning it often, and pressing it down with a broad wooden spoon or flat ladle; when done, drain it through a sieve, pressing out all the moisture, till you get it as dry as you can; then put it on a flat dish, and chop or mince it well; set it again over the fire; add to it some bits of butter dredged with flour and some beaten yolk of egg; let it simmer five minutes or more and when it comes to a boil take it off; have ready some thin slices of buttered toast cut into triangular or three cornered pieces, without any crust; lay them in regular order round a flat dish, and heap the spinach evenly upon them smoothing the surface with the back of a spoon, and scoring it across in diamonds.

Spinach, Mrs. Markrae

Cut off all the stalks. If the leaves are very large cut out the veins also; put with 2 tablespoons salt in a vessel of boiling water enough to well cover it. The vessel to be uncovered. Boil ¼ an hour; put in a colander and as the hot water pours off, pour cold water on; press till not a drop of water remains. Put on a board and chop as fine as possible, mixing black pepper with it as you chop so as to get it well mixed in; put in a sauce pan with a small tea cup of cream and a piece of butter; stew nearly an hour and serve very hot, and garnish with 3 cornered bread fried brown in butter.

- *Carrots*

The carrot is a root that has many good properties not generally known. One or two large raw carrots, washed and grated will greatly improve beef or mutton soup. Sliced thin and boiled with tomatoes, they add a pleasant sweetness to that rather acid vegetable, when prepared for sauce. A raw carrot sliced inside a wild duck and boiled with it will entirely remove the sedgy or fishy taste of the bird. When the duck is half boiled, previous to roasting, take out the carrot, which will have drawn out all the obnoxious taste, and throw it away. Then roast the duck. A poultice of scraped carrot, applied in time, is said to prevent the lockjaw. Radishes make an excellent dish, boiled and dressed like asparagus.

Okra a la Maulie

With 2 tablespoons of butter, fry in a pot 3 slices of ham, 3 sliced onions, until onions are brown. Add 1 quart of young okra, 12 ripe tomatoes from which extract the juice and seeds. Add now the juice and a tumbler of water. Simmer over a slow fire for 3 hours. Thicken with flour and season with salt and pepper.

Yeast, Mrs. Manning

Take a small handful of hops and boil in a qt of water; boil 4 white potatoes and mash as fine as possible, and boil them a few minutes; mix a gill of flour in a little water as a thickening and add to the other ingredients while boiling. Then take off and add a teacup of brown sugar; let it get milk warm, then add 1 gill of former yeast; place the whole in a bottle and set in a warm place to ferment; put the cork in but not tight if the bottle is ½ full at first; when it has risen to ⅔'s, cork and put away.

❦ DESSERTS ❧
Apple, Plum, Blackberry, and Raisin Dishes

- *Apples*

To keep Apples for Winter Use: Put them in casks or bins in layers, well covered with dry sand, each layer being covered; this preserves them from the air, from moisture and from frost; it prevents their perishing by their own perspiration, their moisture being absorbed by the sand; at the same time it preserves the flavor of the apples and prevents their wilting.

Pippins have been kept in this manner sound and fresh till mid-summer, and how much longer they would have kept is not known. Any kind of sand will answer but it must be perfectly dry.

Apple Pudding

Peel and core 8 apples. Grate a quantity of bread crumbs. Place the apples in a baking dish and fill the cores with either jelly or brown sugar. Fill in around and over the apples with bread crumbs interspersed with pieces of butter. Sprinkle brown sugar, cinnamon and a very little wine over the top. Bake and serve with wine sauce.

Charlotte of Apples

Cut some thin slices of bread, dip them in melted butter. Line a well buttered dish or pan bottom and sides with the bread. Cut some apples into a saucepan with a clove. Cover to keep in the steam. Then stew gently until they become soft. Add sugar to taste, candied lemon peel and orange peel. Let all stew one hour. Cover top of pan with one slice of bread well buttered and bake one hour.

Plum Pudding

Mix together 1 lb cleaned currants, 1½ lbs seeded and chopped raisins, ½ lb thinly sliced citron and 1 gill flour; pour 1 quart boiling milk over 1 lb bread, broken in small pieces, cover tightly; cream together 1 lb butter, 1 lb sugar, 1 tsp nutmeg, and 1 tsp cinnamon. Add 9 eggs well beaten. Then add bread and milk and 1 wine glass brandy, whiskey or sherry or 2 tsp vanilla. Add fruit and beat well. Fill 1 lb cans three-fourths full of mixture and cover. Steam 3 hours. Or tie in greased and floured pudding cloth and boil in large saucepan 4 hours. [A gill is equal to 4 oz., and a wine cup is equal to 2 fl. oz.]

Mincemeat

One lb raisins seeded and cut fine, 1 lb apples chopped fine, 1 lb sugar, ½ lb butter, 1 tablespoon powdered cinnamon, 1 nutmeg, 2 wine glasses of brandy or three of wine. In mixing melt the butter and pour it in. Bake in paste.

Eve's Pudding

Currants, grated bread, 6 oz sugar, 6 eggs, 6 apples chopped fine, mix and put in a scalded and floured cloth. Boil 3 hours.

Whortleberry Pudding[15]

One pt milk, 3 eggs and flour enough to make a stiff batter. Stir well together and add 3 pts. berries. Flour a cloth. Tie pretty close, and boil 2 hours and 1/2. Try blackberry and apple pudding as above. Serve with Hard Sauce.

Boiled Blackberry Pudding[16]

One pt flour, 1 tablespoon butter, 1/2 teaspoon yeast, 1 pt milk, 1 qt berries, pinch salt. Make a batter of flour, butter, yeast, and milk. Stir in fruit. Flour towel, tie up tight and boil two hours. Serve with butter sauce.

Plum Cake

Two cups butter, 2 cups molasses, 2 eggs, 1 cup milk, 1 teaspoon volat de salts, 1 gill brandy, nutmeg and flour to make stiff batter. Beat well, then add 1 lb raisins stoned and chopped and 1 lb currants, washed and dried. Bake in quick oven.

---

15. A whortleberry is an indigo-blue berry grown in England and is smaller and tarter than the blueberry.
16. Blackberries grow in abundance in the low country. Emily used them in jams, puddings, cakes, and to make wine and cordials.

Blackberry Cake

Five eggs, 3 cups of sugar, 2 cups butter, 1 teaspoon soda dissolved in a cup of sour milk. Beat the eggs and sugar together, cream the butter and add to it 6 cups flour by degrees; add to it the sugar and eggs gradually till well mixed in. Season with cinnamon, mace or nutmeg. When well mixed stir in two cups preserved blackberries. This makes a good dessert eaten hot with wine sauce.

Cakes and Cookies

Thin Ginger Cake

One half pt molasses, 2 eggs, 1 tablespoon ginger, 1 teaspoon salt, 1/2 lb sugar, 1/2 lb butter, 1 tablespoon cinnamon, 1 dessert spoon cloves. Rub up sugar and butter, add eggs and other ingredients. Put enough plain flour to make thick enough to spread real thin and bake in a medium oven. Cut in squares while hot for it is very crisp when cold.

Ginger Cake

One fourth lb sugar, 1 lb flour, 1/4 lb butter, 1 pt molasses. Rub butter and sugar together. Add molasses and flour and ginger preserves to taste. Bake on tin sheets and spread very thin. Bake quickly. [A pound of sugar or a pound of flour equals 3 1/4 cups.]

Thin Cake

One egg, 1/2 pt sugar, 1 pt flour, 1 large spoonful butter. Rub together egg, sugar and butter. Add flour, if too soft to handle add more. Press out very thin on sheet or pan, sprinkle well with sugar and cinnamon. Bake in moderately hot oven and cut into squares while hot.

Jumbles

Three fourths lb flour, 1/2 lb sugar, 1/4 lb butter, 2 egg whites, 1/2 nutmeg, 1 glass peach water. Cream butter and sugar, add flour and nutmeg gradually with peach water. Fold in whites beaten stiffly. Roll them in sugar and bake on tin sheets. Shape in finger lengths by hand and join so as to make a circle. [A pound of flour equals 3¼ cups of flour.]

Soft Ginger Bread

One half lb butter, 2 cups brown sugar, 3 eggs, 1 glass whiskey, 1 lb flour, ½ pt molasses, mace, nutmeg, cloves, 1 tablespoon ginger, 1 teaspoon soda in cup of milk. Cream butter and sugar till light and add eggs one at a time, then molasses and whiskey. Sift flour and lastly soda and milk. Bake until it leaves the tin.

Husted Cake

One lb flour, 1 lb sugar, ½ lb butter, 6 eggs, 2 teaspoonsful of cream of tartar, one teaspoon of soda, 1 teacup of milk. Flavor with lemon. Beat the yolks and sugar well together; Add the butter which must be creamed, the whites and flour add alternatively. Sift the cream of tartar in the flour, dissolve the soda in the milk and add last. This baked in thin pans makes a nice jelly cake.

Custards and Creams[17]

Real Ice Cream

To 1 qt good cream, add a pt of fresh or boiled milk. Sweeten by essence[18] to taste.

---

17. There are fifteen missing desserts that can be identified from the index but are on pages that have come out. They are: Apple Potato Pudding; Bavarian Cream; Bishops Pudding; Blancmange, Miss Harleston; Blancmange, Mrs. Henry; Bread Pudding Meringue; Buttermilk Curds; Chocolate Custard; Custards; French Custard; Fruit Pies; Omelette Souffle; Pumpkin Pies; Rice Blancmange; and Rice Pudding Meringue.
18. Essence is probably vanilla.

Cream Merangue, Mrs. Sitgreaves

Five yolks, ¼ lb sugar, 1 pt cream, rind of a lemon; Set in boiling water and when thick and cold, beat the whites with sugar and cinnamon; put on the cream and brown.

Charlotte Russe

Put 1 oz Coopers Isinglass[19] previously soaked in cold water into ½ pt milk with a vanilla bean. Then over a slow fire and when the Isinglass is dissolved strain and when luke warm add 4 eggs well beaten. Add ½ lb Sugar. Take 3 pts sweet cream, whip very light, add to the eggs and Isinglass stirring all the time. Put in mounds heaped with sponge cake as soon as mixed. [One package of gelatin soaked in cold water equals 1 oz Isinglass.]

Spanish Cream

Six eggs, 1 gill sugar, 1 qt and ½ milk, 1 oz Coopers Isinglass. Put the ½ pint milk on the Isinglass and let it stand an hour. Then pour on the rest of the milk boiling hot. Add the yolks of eggs and sugar well beaten and let it come to a boil. Flavor to taste and pour into wet moulds. Serve cold with cream.

Trifle

Fill the bottom of a large dish with cake broken into small pieces and moisten with a little wine. Put 1 quart of cream into a deep bowl and

---

19. Artemas Ward, *The Encyclopedia of Food* (New York, 1923), s.v. "isinglass." Isinglass or fish gelatin is a tough, whitish, translucent substance prepared from the bladder of the sturgeon cod. It is employed in the household in the preparation of jellies, blancmange, and similar desserts. Gelatin from animal tissue has, however, largely supplanted it in cookery. Emily's receipts use isinglass, while the later receipts of Anne Sinkler and Anne Fishburne use gelatin.

sweeten to taste with very fine sugar. Beat the whites of 2 eggs very stiff in another vessel and add to the cream. Then churn to stiff froth which as it rises, skim off and put on cake. It must be beaten in a cool place.

Puddings and Pudding Sauces

Quick Sally Lunn

One large tablespoon butter, 2 teaspoons sugar, 4 eggs, 1 quart flour, 1 cup milk, 2 teaspoons baking powder, 1 teaspoon salt. Rub yolks and sugar together till very light. Add milk. Sift in flour to which has been added baking powder and salt, and lastly the stiffly beaten whites of the eggs. Bake in a moderate oven.

• Sally Lunn[20]

I am tempted to send my receipt for this most delicious tea bread, which once eaten at your table, will cause your friends to rejoice when asked to come again: Take a stone pot, pour in one pint bowl of sweet milk, half a teacup of bakers or other yeast, one quarter of a pound of melted butter, a little salt, and three beaten eggs. Mix in about three pint bowls of flour. Let it stand several hours, or until quite light; then put it into Turk heads or other tin pans, in which Sally should again rise up before being shoved into the oven, to be brought out and presented to your friends as the beauty and belle of the evening.—Corres. Country Gentleman.

---

20. Herbst, *Food Lover's Companion,* s.v. "Sally Lunn." Sally Lunn is a rich, slightly sweet yeast bread that may have originated in Bath, England, where it was served as large buns, split horizontally and slathered with clotted cream.

Baked Indian Pudding

Boil 3 pts milk; while boiling stir in enough Indian meal[21] to make it thick as batter cake. Let it cool; when cool beat 6 eggs, add to the batter with enough molasses to sweeten it; bake in a slow oven 1 hour and ½. Dress with a sauce of sweetened cream and nutmeg. [Indian meal is cornmeal.]

French Rice Pudding, Mrs. Markive

One small tea cup sugar; 3 pts milk; nutmeg to the taste; 5 eggs; 1 tbspf Rosewater, little cinnamon, ¼ lb butter. Boil the rice in the milk till quite soft. Beat the yolks till light. Add to the rice mixture. Beat egg whites till stiff and fold into rice mixture. Bake in moderate oven.

Old Time Rice Pudding

To 1 quart of milk add 4 tspfuls sugar, 4 spoonsful unwashed rice, 2 spoonsful butter and 4 eggs with a few pieces of stick cinnamon added. Bake in moderate oven until rice is soft.

Bread Pudding

A small slice of bread soaked in 1 quart of boiling milk. When cold beat up with 1 spoonful butter, 4 eggs, sugar to taste, nutmeg or cinnamon. Bake in moderate oven.

Baked Batter Pudding

Eight eggs, 1 pt flour, 1 quart milk. Beat eggs light, add flour and milk, pour in pan and grate nutmeg over it. Bake quickly and serve hot with butter sauce.

---

21. Indian meal, or cornmeal, is here combined with molasses and eggs to form a baked pudding.

Sweet Potato Pudding

One lb boiled sweet potatoes, 1 lb sugar, 1 wine glass wine, 4 eggs, 1/2 cup milk, 1 tsp grated nutmeg. Smoothly mash potatoes. Rub sugar and butter together, then add 2 egg whites and 4 egg yolks. Add milk and wine. Bake in pudding pan in moderate oven. Make meringue with 2 remaining whites beaten up with 4 tablespoons sugar. Put on meringue while pudding is hot and put back in oven for few minute to brown.

Lemon Pudding

One half lb bread crumbs, 1 pint milk, grated rind of 1 lemon, 1 cup sugar, yolks of 2 eggs, juice of half lemon. Beat yolks until light, add sugar and bread crumbs which have been soaked in milk, then juice and rind of lemon. Bake until thick. Beat whites stiff, add sugar and flavor with lemon, then put meringue on top. Put in oven and brown.

Sweet Potato Pone

One quart grated potato, 1/2 pt molasses, 10 oz sugar, 10 oz butter, 3 eggs. Cream butter and sugar, add eggs. Add grated potato gradually with molasses.

Wine Sauce for Puddings

Fill a teacup with brown sugar. Pour as much wine upon it as it will hold. Melt it with a little butter, nutmeg and cinnamon stirred in.

Hard Sauce

Beat to a cream one cup butter to which add 3 cups sugar. Beat long and hard. Then place in dish, smooth and sprinkle with nutmeg. Flavor with wine.

Pudding Sauce

One tablespoon of flour, stirred smoothly into a bit of butter the size of an egg; one half pint of sugar, worked in; the grated peel and juice of a lemon; one half pint of warm water. Let it boil, take it off; let it cool a little, and stir in both yolk and white of a well beaten egg.

❦ BREAD AND WARM CAKES[22] ❧
Bread and Muffins from Indian Meal

Bannocks[23]

Boil 1 pt milk and pour on 1 pt Indian meal.[24] Beat well the yolk of 4 eggs, and mix with 1 pt cold milk; then add the whites of the eggs, 1 teaspoon soda and a little salt. Bake.

Indian Cakes, Mrs. Flox

One qt milk, ¼ lb butter, 1 pt Indian meal, 6 eggs. Boil the milk and butter together; pour over the meal to which has been added 1 tsp salt. Let stand 2 or 3 hours and add the eggs well beaten, leaving out the whites of 4, and add about 5 even tablespoons wheat flour; add more milk if too stiff.

---

22. There are fifteen missing bread and warm cake receipts that can be identified from the index but are on pages that have fallen out. They are: Burlington Cakes, Buttermilk Cake, Corn Biscuits, Covington Cake, Doughnuts, German Pudding, German Sponge Cake, Gingerbread Pound Cake, Jelly Cake, Manning Biscuits, Mrs. Sitgreave's Cake, Rice Bread, Soda Cakes, Tea Bread, and Tea Cake.
23. Herbst, *Food Lover's Companion*, s.v. "bannock." This is a traditional Scottish cake, usually made with barley meal or oatmeal. They were often served at high tea. Here Emily makes them with Indian meal.
24. Ward, *The Encyclopedia of Food*, s.v. "Indian meal." Indian meal is a term for cornmeal.

Virginia Corn Bread

Rub a piece of butter size of egg into 1 pt corn meal; make into a batter with some new milk and 2 eggs, add some yeast; set by the fire for an hour; butter some pans and bake.

Bread, Rolls, Pancakes, and Waffles from Wheat Flour

Bunns

Three cups milk, 1 cup yeast, 1 sugar and flour enough to make a stiff batter. Let it rise over night. In the morning add 1 cup butter, 1 sugar, 1 nutmeg, and teaspoon Saleratus and flour the bread. Let it rise again and then cut out, and let stand while the oven is preparing.

• Flannel Cakes

Mrs. Swisshelm says: To make flannel cakes, take two eggs for a quart of sour milk, a table spoonful of melted butter, one of sugar, and half a one of salt. Put all together without beating the eggs. Mix it into a batter stiff enough to drop off a spoon like an oyster. Then have some saleratus dissolved in water, and stir in slowly until your batter begins to rise. Be careful not to put in enough to turn the color. If the milk is only sour enough to thicken, a teaspoon full of saleratus is enough for the quart; if it has fermented it may require two and your cakes will be nicer. Have a griddle hot, and bake like buckwheat.

• Lime Water in Bread

It has lately been found that water saturated with lime produces in bread the same whiteness, softness and capacity of retaining moisture, as results from the use of alum while the former removes all acidity from the dough, and supplies an ingredient needed in the structure of the bones, but which is deficient in the cerealia.

Rolls, Mrs. Manning

To 1 qt flour mix a large spoonful butter, a little salt and a large tablespoon yeast; then beat up 2 eggs; mix them with as much new milk as will make the whole of a right consistency; cover and set to rise; in the morning separate into rolls; set again to rise and bake.

Bread, Mrs. Devaux

Boil the water in warm weather. Let it be cold in cold weather. Warm milk, and add a small piece of butter; knead until it does not stick; for rolls boil the milk and let it cool.

Bread, Mrs. Manning

Sift 3 pts flour; put in a bowl; make a hole in the middle; add 3 iron spoons of yeast, 1 teaspoon salt and enough water to make it stiff, reserving a little flour on side of the bowl; cover it, warm and set to rise; let it rise from 6 to 7 hours; knead it up into a loaf with the rest of the flour; put it into the bread pan and let it rise again and bake.

Receipt for Bread from EB's book

To 1 qt warm water put a gill good yeast; stir in flour to make a thin batter and let it stand in a warm place all night. Next morning put 7 lbs flour in a wooden tray, make hollow in middle. Add to the sponge a bit of volatile salts size of single alum; nutmegs dissolved in warm water and a piece of alum size of a hickory nut, finely powdered; stir with spoon till it is a light foam, then pour into the hollow of flour. Add a heaping tablespoon salt and a qt or more of warm water.

Delicate Cake

One and 1/2 cups sugar. The same of flour. One half cup each of butter, milk and cornstarch. The whites of 6 eggs. One teaspoon cream of tartar, 1/2 teaspoon soda.

Sally Lippincott's Cake

One fourth lb butter; ¼ lb sugar; ½ lb flour; 2 eggs and milk to mix into a soft dough. Teaspoon soda, 1 tablespoon orange flower water. Put the butter into flour. Add a little salt to taste.

Pendleton Rusk

One cup yeast, 2 of milk, 3 of flour. Put in the oven over night. In the morning add three eggs, 2 cups sugar, and flour enough to make a stiff dough. Knead and put in pans in hot oven.

Rusk, Mrs. Porcher

One pint yeast made into leaven, when sufficiently risen, take 4 eggs, 1 spoonful butter, ½ pt milk; 1 and ½ pts sugar. Beat these all well together, then add flour till the spoon will stand in it; put it to rise. When sufficiently risen knead it into rolls and let it rise again. Mix the batter about 12 o'clock, and at bed time it will be sufficiently risen to add the other ingredients.

Sweet Wafers, Mrs. Porcher

One egg, 1 spoonful butter, 1 of sugar and 2 of flour, well beaten. A little nutmeg.

Macaroons

One lb blanched, beaten almonds. 1 lb sugar. The whites of 4 eggs well beaten. A little Rosewater. Drop on paper and bake directly in a moderate oven.

Ginger Cake

One and ¾ lbs flour, 1 pt molasses, ¼ lb ginger, 1 lb sugar, ½ lb butter, ½ lb citron. Rub sugar and butter together. Add molasses and ginger. Sift in flour and citron.

Seed Cake

Two lbs of flour; 1 lb of sugar; 2 lbs of butter; a little caraway seed; 1 teaspoonfull of salerated dillseed in milk; ½ pint of milk. To be rolled out thin and baked in a quick oven. [On a letter signed E.W.F.]

Sweet Waffles

Six eggs, ¼ lb butter, 1½ lb flour, 1 pint milk, ½ lb white sugar, 1 teaspoon cinnamon. Warm milk. Cut up butter in it and beat eggs well and pour in the milk. Sprinkle in half the flour. Gradually stir in the sugar and spice by degrees. Then add gradually the rest of flour until it becomes thick. When the waffles are done spread them separately on a towel. When the plate is full, butter them and sprinkle cinnamon over them.

Soda Biscuit, Mary Ann Fora

One teaspoon soda, 2 teaspoons cream of tartar, 1 teaspoon butter, 1 qt flour; mix the cream of tartar into the flour which has been first sifted and a little shaken out for kneading; dissolve the soda and add to it not quite a pt milk; stir into the flour; add the butter, and a little salt; knead a little; cut into round cakes and bake 20 minutes. One rule says 5 teaspoons cream of tartar, 2 of soda.

Biscuits

One pint flour, 1 gill milk, 1 heaping tablespoon butter, 1 heaping teaspoon baking powder. Rub butter, salt and baking powder into the flour. Roll out on a biscuit board about ½ inch thick. Cut with biscuit cutter and bake in hot oven.

Mountain Cake

One cup of butter, 2 of sugar, 3 of flour, 1 of milk and six eggs. 1 teaspoon cream of tartar mixed with flour. ½ teaspoon soda put in dry the last thing.

Mountain Cake, Mrs. Lewis

One half pt sour cream, very small teaspoon saleratus,[25] more than 1 lb flour; a piece of butter size egg. Mix flour and butter together. Dissolve the saleratus well in the cream, mixing first in a spoonful separately; then in all the cream; stir into the flour and butter. Roll out with a little flour, make thicker than for pie crust. Bake 10 minutes in a quick oven; roll very little.

Flannel Cakes, Mrs. Flox

Three pts milk, 3 pts flour, 8 eggs, lump of butter size of egg and yeast.

Bread from Rice and Rice Flour

Rice Cakes, Mrs. Gaillard

Mix 4 large spoonfuls soft boiled rice; 1 spoonful butter, 2 eggs and 1 gill milk together; stir in rice flour; form into little round cakes and bake.

Rice Cakes, Mrs. Lewis

Boil ½ pt rice soft; mix with it 3 gills flour and a little salt; 2 oz melted butter; 2 eggs beaten well and as much milk as will make a thick batter; beat till very light.

Rice Scones

One half pint flour, 1 cup boiled rice, 1 full tablespoon baking powder, 1 cup milk, 1 teaspoon salt, 2 tablespoon butter. Add salt and powder to flour and sift. Rub in butter and rice. Gradually mix with milk. This must be soft enough to drop from a spoon. Dip spoon into boiling water and drop dough on a greased pan. Bake in quick oven.

---

25. Saleratus or soda saleratus is one of the chief ingredients of all baking powder.

- *Receipt for Rice Bread*[26]

To one pint Rice Flour add one pint Clabber, sour milk, butter milk or sweet milk acidulated, a little Salt, papspoonful of butter or cream, with half a teaspoonful of Saleratus or cooking soda; stir the latter with the liquid, mix well and rapidly, and put in a greased pan. Eat with fresh butter, just from the churn, if you want it in perfection; but should your taste have been vitiated by life in the city, and your Patriotism will permit use the best Northern, if you can get it. Should your feelings for the Yankee article be too strong however, you will find syrup or honey quite tolerable. Yours QUINCUNX

Mrs. Gordon's Cornbread

One gill raw rice; 2 gills milk; 3 eggs; ½ gill corn flour; 1 tablespoon butter.

Bread from Potatoes

Margaret Hart's Potato Cakes

Take ½ a doz potatoes. Peel and boil. Mash them soft with some salt. Add ½ a pint hot milk and ¼ lb butter dissolved in it. When cool add about a teacupfull of home made yeast and flour enough for a soft dough. Set to rise; when light cut into small cakes and let them rise again. Then bake in a quick oven.

---

26. Karen Hess, *The Carolina Rice Kitchen: The African Connection* (Columbia: University of South Carolina Press, 1992), p. 116. Rice bread tends to be dense and tends not to rise because rice is deficient in gluten. Emily used boiled rice, as well as combining rice flour with Indian meal. Boiled rice works well in making a good loaf as it does not dilute the gluten content of wheat flour.

❦ SUNDRY RECIPES ❧
Pasta

Maccaroni, Mrs. Lamae

Put in boiling water in a vessel large enough to allow it to swell, with a blade of mace and 1 teaspoon of salt; must boil ¾ hour, then take out and make the following sauce. Half a teacup cream, 1 teaspoon flour, the yolk of an egg and 2 teaspoons salt and a small piece of butter; beat up well; pour over the maccaroni; grate cheese over. Brown, and serve.

Maccaroni and Tomato

Boil the maccaroni until soft. Strain. Stew the tomatoes with butter and flour until as thick as a fricassee sauce. Then mix with maccaroni, salt and pepper to taste and bake for half an hour.

Maccaroni, Mrs. Gaillard

Boil in water till it swells; strain off the water and add sufficient milk to cover it; let it boil till soft; add a little salt, 1 tablespoon butter, 2 teaspoons made mustard; put half in a pan and grate cheese over them; add the other half, cover the tops with cheese and bake ½ hour.

Vermicelli, Mrs. Randolph

Beat 2 or 3 fresh eggs till quite light; make them into a stiff paste with flour; Knead well, roll out very thin, cut in narrow strips and dry quickly on tin sheets.[14]

---

14. Mary Randolph, *The Virginia House-wife, with Historical Notes and Commentaries by Karen Hess* (Columbia: University of South Carolina Press, 1994), p. 100. Emily faithfully attributes this receipt to Mary Randolph, whose cookbook was first published in 1824. Emily owned a copy of Mrs. Randolph's cookbook and used it.

Butter and Cheese

Orange County Butter

Strain the milk into clean pans; allow it to stand till it is clotted at the bottom of the pans; 36 hours is the usual time. Keep your pans very scrupulously neat and clean. Any impurities in the air will have a bad effect on the cream. When you take off the cream put it in a stone jar unless you have enough to skim every day. Scald the churn and dasher thoroughly filling the former afterwards with cold water, then throw it out. Put in a tumbler of fresh water, in winter warm, in summer cold. Then pour in the cream. In churning the motion should be regular and moderate so that the temperature may be uniform through all. When the butter curdles and forms in the churn, a glass or two of water to aid in gathering the butter. Previously scald the butter bowl and ladle and leave cold water standing in the bowl. Take the butter into it and wash it in water. When the buttermilk forms take out the butter.

• *Mock Cream*

Mock cream may be made by mixing half a table spoonful of flour with a pint of new milk, letting it simmer five minutes to take off the rawness of the flour; beat up the yolk of an egg, stir it into the milk while boiling and run it through a fine sieve.

Elizabeth's Cottage Cheese

Take a pan of thick milk. In winter put it near the fire; let it stand about an hour or so to warm all through but not scald; when the whey separates and it is about $1/2$ whey, put a thick cloth on the sieve and let it drain through. Then put a plate on the clabber and 2 flat irons on it. Let it stand about 6 or 8 hours to press. Then take a plate full, mash soft, add salt and sweet cream to thin it, about a tea cup.

- *Potato Cheese*

Potato Cheese is celebrated in various parts of Europe. It is made thus: Boil good white potatoes and when cold, peel them and rasp or mash them to a light pulp; to five pounds of this which must be free from lumps add a pint of sour milk, and salt to taste; knead the whole well, cover it and leave it for two or three days according to the season; then knead it afresh, and put the cheese into small baskets, when they will part with the superfluous moisture; dry them in the shade and place them in layers in large pots or kegs where they may remain a fortnight. The older they are the finer they become.

Drawn Butter

One fourth lb. butter and 1 tablespoon flour; work them well together; put in a sauce pan and pour on hot water and stir till the butter is dissolved; put it where it will get warm; it must not boil.

Preserves and Jellies

Grape Preserves

Weigh fruit, separate pulps and skins. Boil pulps until soft and mash through vegetable masher to get out seeds. Put skins with enough water to boil them and boil till soft. Add sugar and pulps and boil till jellied. The proportion of sugar is ¾ lb to 1 lb of fruit.

Blackberry Jam

Weigh berries before washing and to every pound of fruit put ¾ lb of sugar. Do not put any water. Boil until of desired consistency.

Crab Apple Jelly

Cut apples in half and soak over night in enough water to cover them. Then to a cup of juice add a cup of sugar. Strain and boil till jellied.

112

Fig Preserves

Gather good ripe firm figs. Wash figs in lime water, allowing them to soak a few minutes. Then rinse in clear water. To 8 pound of figs put 5 pounds of sugar. Put in skillet with the sugar without any water and boil till figs are clear. Put into jars while real hot and screw down at once.

Spiced Figs

Wash figs in plain cold water. Do not put lime on them or peel them. Put sugar on figs over night to let them draw juice. Vinegar may be put on at night, or added in the morning. Put 5 pounds of sugar to seven pounds of figs. The figs must be ripe and firm. To a peck of figs put one and one half pints of vinegar. A good handful each of cloves and allspice. Let boil until figs are clear. Put in jars and seal.

Watermelon Rind Preserves

Pare the rind thin and cut in forms. Put in cold salt and water for 24 hours, then in alum water, allowing 1 oz of alum[27] to 1 gallon of water for 24 hours. Then in cold water until the alum is extracted. Then boil a syrup with 1 1/4 pounds of sugar to every pound of rind. When the syrup becomes clear, put in the rind and let them boil until perfectly clear. Several pints of water may be added as the syrup boils away. Flavor with lemon or ginger.

Quince Preserves

Cut the quinces in half and put them in a kettle of water. Boil until quite tender. When cool pare and core them. Put a pound of sugar to

---

27. *American Heritage Dictionary,* 2nd college ed., s.v. "alum." Alum was used in cooking as a hardening or clarifying agent.

every pound of fruit and make a syrup of the water the quinces were boiled in, allowing a pint to each pound of sugar. When that is cold put in the quinces with a few pickling spices and boil until transparent.

Pear Chips

Eight quarts peeled and sliced pears, 7 lbs sugar, 3 oranges, 2 lemons, 2 oz ginger root. Dissolve sugar in 1 pint water. Add pears and grated lemons and oranges, also ginger cut small. Boil till chips are clear. Jar while hot.

Peach Chips

To 12 lbs peaches add 6 lbs sugar. Make a syrup and put the peaches in. Cut in thin slices. Simmer over a gentle fire till they look clear. Take from the fire and let them remain off for the night. Then take out and put in a sieve to drain perfectly dry. Pack away in powdered sugar.

Brandy Peaches

Pick out the fairest peaches. Peel very thin and throw into cold water. One and ½ pints of water to 3 pounds of sugar will boil 8 pounds of peaches. When cold put into jars and fill the jars with whiskey or brandy.

To Keep Preserves

Apply the white of egg with a brush to a single thickness of white tissue paper, with which cover the jars, over lapping the edge an inch or 2; no tying required; when dry will be as tight as a drum.

• Ludlow & Co's Self Sealing Can

First select good fresh fruit or vegetables; fermented articles can never be preserved. Vegetables decomposing such as green corn, green peas, asparagus, should be preserved within six hours after being picked, particularly in hot weather; berries always within twenty four hours. Peaches, quinces, pears, apples should be pealed and the seed removed before preserving. To preserve unripe berries and fruits, and vegetables, boil twice while in the cans. Vegetables should be partially cooked first, such as corn, peas, and tomatoes, should be boiled a half hour; asparagus a quarter hour. To the vegetables add a half pint of the water they are cooked in to the quart. Place them in the cans and after securing down the cap with the fingers put the cans in boiling water and boil asparagus 1 hour; and green peas, corn or beans three hours. Then unscrew the caps, leaving them off two minutes, then the cap should again be secured on and fastened tightly with the wrench made for the purpose, and boil again, the asparagus for 30 minutes, and the green peas, corn or beans for 3 hours.

- *To Make Good Apple Jelly*

Take apples of the best quality and good flavor, not sweet; cut them in quarters or slices, and stew them till soft; then strain out the juice being very careful not to let any of the pulp go through the strainer. Boil it to the consistency of molasses, then weigh it and add as many pounds of crushed sugar, stirring it constantly till the sugar is dissolved. Add one ounce of extract of lemon to every twenty pounds of jelly and when cold set it away in closed jars and it will keep good for years.

Candy

Hot Icing, Mrs. Manning

Put 1 wine glass water and 1 wine glass Rosewater over 1 lb finely beaten loaf sugar; while dissolving beat the whites of 4 eggs very light. Put the sugar on the fire to heat, not to boil and mix the eggs in very gradually; must be beaten all the time and quickly. Pour in a bowl and continue beating with a spoon a short time. A small quantity of Isinglass or gum Arabic mixed with the water before it is poured on the sugar makes it more glassy.

Toast Candy

To 3 lbs loaf sugar just add ½ pint water. Set it over a slow fire for ½ an hour. Then add a teaspoon gum Arabic dissolved and a tablespoon vinegar. When boiled to a candy take off and flavor. Rub the hands with sweet butter and pull till white; make in rolls and cut in lengths.

Chocolate Caramels

One fourth lb chocolate, 2 cups sugar, ¼ cup butter, ½ cup milk. Break chocolate into milk. When dissolved boil for ½ hour, stirring for awhile until it can form a soft ball in water. Add 1 teaspoon flavoring. Pour in buttered dish and cut into squares when cool.

Chocolate Candy

One cup sweet milk, 1 cup molasses, ½ cup sugar, ½ cup grated chocolate, butter size of walnut. Mix and stir constantly. Let boil until thick. Turn out on buttered plates. When it begins to stiffen mark in squares so it will break readily when cold.

Bene Candy[28]

Four tumblers sugar, 1 tumbler water, 1 tumbler vinegar, 2 tumblers bene seed. Stir all together and when boiled pour out thin on greased tin pans.

---

28. Herbst, *Food Lover's Companion,* s.v. "sesame seed." Sesame seed is widely used in southern cooking for candy and for wafers. Sesame seed was called "bene" seed in Africa and came to the United States as a result of the slave trade. The tiny, flat seed has a nutty, slightly sweet flavor.

Groundnut Macaroons

One pt parched and ground groundnuts,[29] 1 pt sugar, white of 3 eggs beaten stiff. Add alternately to the beaten egg whites, the sugar and ground nuts. Either drop in spoonfuls or spread on a tin, and bake till a pretty brown. Cut while hot.

Beverages

Pineapple Champagne

To the rind of 1 pineapple cut in small pieces, add 2 qts clear water. Tie a piece of thin cloth over the bowl, and leave it to ferment, which it will in a day; as the fermentation subsides strain and sweeten to your taste. Bottle in strong bottles and tie down the corks. Will be risen in 48 hours. Lay the bottles on their sides.

Lady's Book Blackberry Wine[30]

Measure the berries and bruise. To every gallon add a qt boiling water. Let it stand 24 hours stirring occasionally. Strain into a cask adding to cask gallon 2 lbs sugar. Cork tight and let remain till October.

---

29. *American Heritage Dictionary,* 2nd college ed., s.v. "groundnuts." Groundnuts are the nutlike tuber of a climbing vine, *Apios tuberosa.* Groundnuts as used above are probably peanuts, which have a long tradition in low country cooking.
30. Emily Fishburne Whaley relates this story. Each May, Anne "Nan" Sinkler Fishburne would have her cook, Cat, spread the word that "Miss Anne" wanted blackberries and would pay for them. Pounds of ripe blackberries appeared overnight, and Nan would begin the process of making blackberry wine on the back porch in demijohns, much like the above receipts from her grandmother Emily. For guests Nan always had blackberry wine, which she served in Venetian green wine glasses.

Cousin Dollie's Blackberry Wine

Gather in the ripest blackberries and mash. To a gallon of the fruit put a gallon of water. Pour through a hair sieve or coarse cloth. For a gallon of the liquid add 3 lbs. brown sugar. Pour in French Brandy cask and let it stand for six months. Bung it tight and after it has remained six months suck off in bottles and it is fit for use. The cask should be very nearly or quite full. Cork not in very tight for a few days. Lay the cask on its side.

Mrs. Porcher's Blackberry Wine

Press the berries, put in a stone jar and let them remain 24 hours. Strain off the juice and to every gallon put 1 qt water and 3 lbs brown sugar. Put in a demi john. Cork lightly. Pour off in September or October. Bottle and use in the following March.

Stoughton Bitters

Six oz Orange Peel, 4 oz Gentian Root,[31] ½ oz Snake Root, 4 oz Red Landess. Put in a gallon best brandy. Cut peel very small, but put the Snake root and Red Landess as they are. 2 oz Cinnamon added is an improvement. [Signed, Elizabeth Bast, 1858.]

Plum Brandy

One and ½ lbs plums, 2 lbs sugar, 2 gals brandy. Cover plums with sugar and brandy. Let stand 2 or 3 months. Pour off, strain and bottle.

---

31. *American Heritage Dictionary,* 2nd college ed., s.v. "gentian root." Gentian root has been used as a tonic.

Cherry Bounce

Make same as Plum Brandy, using black cherries instead of plums.

Strawberry Acid

Cover 12 lbs of fruit with 2 quarts water. Add 5 oz of tartaric acid and let it stand 48 hours. Strain through a flannel bag without bruising. To each pint of juice add 1 heavy pound of sugar. Stir until dissolved then leave for 24 hours. Bottle and leave uncorked for 10 days; tie muslin over the top.

Ratifia

To 1 gallon whiskey, put 400 peach kernels, 1 pint orange flower water or orange peel cut fine, 1½ pints of sugar and 1 pint Rosewater. Improves with age.

Hot Tea

Throw in a pinch of Carbonate of soda.[32] Put the tea into the empty pot and put before the fire or in the hot plate of the oven until the tea be well heated but not burnt. Then pour on the boiling water.

Shrub

Take the rind of half a lemon and half an orange pared quite thin. Put in a pint of rum and let it remain three hours when it should be removed. Add to the rum a small wine glass of strained lemon juice and the same of orange juice, 1 ounce of lump sugar, dissolved in a pint and a half of water. Mx all and bottle.

---

32. *American Heritage Dictionary*, 2nd college ed., s.v. "soda." Carbonate of soda is sodium carbonate that produces carbonated water.

French Coffee

Now ground the berries more than an hour before the coffee is prepared, and always roast at least once a week. Put the powder in the Biggin[33] in the proportion of 12 oz to a serving cup full of water. Some say put ½ cup full of powder to the same. Pour on the water which must be boiling, and then keep it on the fire so that it shall be very hot, but under boiling point. This is usually kept thus for 2 hours.

Soups

Elizabeth's Chicken Soup

Wash the fowl, tie up with a twine, put it in a soup pot with 3 qts and 1 pt cold water. Let it simmer slowly for 3 hours. When the scum rises skim it off and then add about ½ a large cup of barley. Can add some pot herbs, with parsley add a small onion cut up fine. Before dishing up, add pepper and salt; at the last beat up the yolks of two and white of one, and add to it ½ tea cup young cream; take the chicken out, pour in the cream very slowly while it is on the fire; must not boil lest the eggs curdle. Rub some pieces of toasted bread in the tureen and pour on it.

Elizabeth's Split Pea Soup[34]

Night before pick and soak 1 pt in cold water; wash them before, so as to keep the water they have been soaked in. In the morning put them in a little more water and let them stew about ½ hour. In the morning put a chicken or some beef in about 2 qts water about nine o'clock. At one

33. *American Heritage Dictionary,* 2nd college ed., s.v. "biggin." A biggin was a coffee percolator used in the early 19th century.
34. Note that Emily combines this with chicken or beef and adds sautéed celery, asparagus, tomato, and onion at the last.

o'clock add the peas. Just before dishing up add ½ pt sweet cream. Have toasted bread in tureen. Pour on soup. After skimming meat, add celery, asparagus, 1 tomato, onion cut up. Season at the last.

Julien Soup, Mrs. Paul

Take a shin of beef. Boil it all day in 5 or 6 quarts of water. Then strain through a colander and put away for next day. Next day boil ½ cup barley, a grated carrot, tomatoes, ochras,[35] celery, an onion, sliced potatoes in lime water for 2 or 3 hours. Scrape off the fat from the stock, warm thoroughly, add the vegetables and boil all together for an hour.

Old Fowl Soup, Mrs. Randolph

Cut off the legs and wings of the fowl; separate the breast from the ribs and put aside with the back. Wash the pieces and put on the fire with about a lb of bacon, a large onion chopped small, some pepper and salt, a handful of parsley chopped fine and 2 qts water. A turkey will take more. Boil gently for 3 hours. Thicken with a large spoonful of butter rubbed into two of flour; the yolks of 2 eggs and ½ pint milk, which be careful not to let curdle.

To Make Winter Pea Soup[36]

Take 1 qt split peas; put them to soak over-night in cold water. Directly after breakfast put them in a pot of boiling water with a piece of salt pork that has been well washed in cold water; add some onion, some celery and a little black pepper. Boil slowly all the morning; when it thickens up add more water till it is about as thick as gruel; before dinner take the soup and skim it. Put back into the pot to keep it hot; have ready some small pieces of fried bread which serve in the soup.

---

35. Okra was and is widely grown in the South, and this is probably a variant spelling.
36. Winter pea soup made with split peas is mentioned on several occasions in Emily's letters.

Eggs

To Keep Eggs

Immerse in boiling water long enough to count 20 at a rapid rate.

To Preserve Eggs

Gypsum or Sulfate of Lime or Lime Water will keep eggs for 6 months or more.

Lime Water

Put a pt of best store Lime in any vessel with a large mouth. Cover it with 2 qts of water. When settled, pour off and bottle up for use. If too strong when used add a little water.

Omelet

Nine eggs beaten well. Add a little salt and pepper, ½ a tea cup milk or cream; add some parsley chopped fine. Melt some butter in a pan. Pour in the mixture. Keep stirring from the sides and bottom till it is sufficiently done; then let it stand a second or so to brown and turn out.

Soyers Omelet

Break four eggs in a bowl. Add ½ teaspoon of salt and ¼ teaspoon pepper. Beat up well with a fork. Put in the frying pan 1 oz and ½ butter. Put on the fire till hot. Then pour in the eggs and keep beating with a spoon till all is delicately set. Then let them slip to the edges of the pan laying hold of the handle and raising it slantways which will give the omelet a loose form. Turn in the edges. Let it set a moment, turn out on a dish and serve. The pans in which omelets are cooked should be free from damp, therefore put it on the fire with a little butter. Let this get hot.

Remove it wiping the pan with a dry cloth and proceed as above. Another way: beat well 6 eggs, 1 teaspoon sweet cream and fry in a pan with melted butter. Heat the pan before pouring in the eggs. During frying, move the pan continually, till it is an inch thick; then hold pan still a moment and then serve.

Lady St. Clair's Omelette

¼ pt cream and the yolks of 6 eggs beaten well together with a little cayenne and salt; then add a small piece of shallot and a little parsley minced very fine. Mix well together. Whip the whites of 5 eggs and stir in the omelette till very light. Melt a little butter in the frying pan and pour in the eggs. Cook over a quick fire for five mins.

Elizabeth's Breakfast Eggs

Boil 6 eggs hard; when cold, split and take out the yolks; put in a dish and make as for salad; chop together fine parsley, salt and pepper, a few bread crumbs and a little butter. If too dry add a little milk or cream; fill the hollow parts of the whites with this mixture; fry in a little butter, first the white side, having previously salted it then the other. Takes very little frying.

❧ HOUSEHOLD FORMULAS ❧
Soaps and Washing

To Make Soap, Mrs. Randolph[37]

Put on the fire any quantity of lye[38] you choose that is strong enough to bear an egg. To each gallon, add ¾ lb of clean grease; boil it very fast,

---

37. Randolph, *The Virginia House-wife,* p. 222. This formula as well as that for making cosmetic soap come from Mrs. Randolph.
38. *American Heritage Dictionary,* 2nd college ed., s.v. "lye." Lye is potassium hydroxide and is obtained by leaching wood ashes.

and stir it frequently. A few hours will suffice to make it good soap. When you find by cooling a little on a plate that it is a thick jelly, and no grease appears, put in salt in the proportions of 1 to 3 gallons. Let it boil a few minutes, and pour in tubs to cook. Should the soap be thin, add a little water to that in the plate. Stir it well, and by that means ascertain how much is necessary for the whole quantity. Very strong lye will require water to thicken it before the salt is added. Next day cut out the soap. Melt it and cool it again. Should cracknels be used, then must be 1 lb to each gallon. Soft soap is made in the same manner omitting the salt. It may also be made by putting lye and grease in exact proportions under the influence of a hot sun 8 or 10 days, stirring it 4 or 5 times a day.

Soap with Concentrated Lye

Dissolve well 1 box lye in 2½ gals water. Add 5 lbs grease and then add gradually 2 gals eau or soft water. Boil hard 20 mins. Then add slowly 1 pt salt which makes a jelly. Boil hard 20 mins longer stirring constantly. Then put away to cool and cut in bars.

Cosmetic Soap, Mrs. Randolph

Take 1 lb. of castile or any other nice old soap; scrape it in small pieces, and put it on the fire with a little water. Stir it till it becomes a smooth paste. Pour it into a bowl, and when cold add some lavender water, or essence of any kind. Beat it with a silver spoon until well mixed. Thicken it with corn meal, and keep it in small pots closely covered. The admission of air will soon make the soap hard.

Potash Soap

Take 6 pounds of Potash. Take 4 pounds of Lard and ¼ pound of Rosin.[39] Beat up the Rosin and mix all well together. Set it aside for five

---

39. *American Heritage Dictionary,* 2nd college ed., s.v. "rosin." Rosin is the sap of pine trees.

days. Then put the whole into a ten gallon cask of warm water and stir twice a day for ten days. At the end of which time you will have 100 pounds of soap.

- *Soap for Washing*

To each pound of common hard soap add ½ oz common borax,[40] pulverized and 1 quart water. Put the water into a tin pan or other convenient vessel and place on the stove; put in the borax, and then add the soap cut in small thin pieces. Keep them hot and not boiling, several hours or until the soap is dissolved. When cool it will be double the quantity and thus save at least one half. Rub the dirtiest part of the clothes with this compound and soak them over night if convenient. This mixture does not cut the hands, and is adapted to all sorts of clothes. They are to be washed, boiled and rinsed as usual but the labor of rubbing is greatly lessened.

- *How to Do Up Shirt Bosoms*

Take two ounces of fine white gum Arabic powder; put it into a pitcher, and pour on it a pint or more of boiling water, and then having covered it let it set all night. In the morning pour it carefully from the dregs into a clean bottle, cork it, and keep it for use. A tablespoonful of gum water, stirred into a pint of starch made in the usual manner, will give to lawns, either white or printed, a look of newness when nothing else can restore them after washing.

To Wash Ribbons

To wash ribbons make a lather of clean white soap, the water as warm as you can bear your hands. Soap may be applied where there are grease

---

40. *American Heritage Dictionary,* 2nd college ed., s.v. "borax." Borax is hydrated sodium borate and is used in the manufacture of glass and ceramics.

spots on the wrong side. As soon as washed have ready a hot iron and press them out. While wet pressing on the wrong side. To stiffen dip in gum Arabic.

To Take Rust from Sheets

Cover with Salad oil, well rubbed in and 48 hours afterwards use powdered unslaked lime[41] and rub till the rust disappears.

Linen

Preparation for Linen before marking: 1 drachma of salts of Tartar[42] dissolved in 1 and $\frac{1}{2}$ oz water.

• To Remove Ink Stains from Cloth

The moment the ink is spilt take a little milk and saturate the stain; soak it up with a rag and apply a little more milk, rubbing it well in. In a few minutes the ink will be completely removed.

To Extract Stains from Black Clothes

Take a handful of fig leaves; boil in 2 quarts water until reduced to 1 pt. Strain and apply to any kind of black stuff.

Flannels

Flannels may be prevented from shrinking if on the first time of washing they are put in a pot, boiling water poured on them and then are allowed to lie till cold.

---

41. *American Heritage Dictionary*, 2nd college ed., s.v. "lime." Unslaked lime is calcium oxide.
42. *American Heritage Dictionary*, 2nd college ed., s.v. "tartar." Salts of tartar are derived from tartaric acid and are used in baking powders.

- *Washing Clothes, a Hint*

Whoever will soak clothes from twenty four to thirty six hours before washing them will find that they can do without patent washing fluids and save nearly all the wear of clothes by rubbing too.

- *Stains in Linens*

For acid stains, wet the part and lay on it salt or wormwood then rub it or let the cloth imbibe water without dripping and hold the part over a lighted match for the sulphurous gas; or tie up pearl ash in the stained part; scrape soap into cold water for a lather and boil the linen till the stains disappear.

Cleaning Formulas

- *Use Copperas*

The papers are everywhere urging the free use of copperas[43] as a disinfecting agent. It is a cheap article, costing only three cents per pound and can be found at the druggists and many of the larger grocery stores. A couple of pounds may be dissolved in ten quarts of water, and the solution poured into sinks, gutters, cesspools, and all other filthy places with good effect. Cholera[44] or no cholera dwelling and out buildings will contain a purer atmosphere after the use of copperas.

- *Tea Kettles*

To prevent tea kettles coating with lime, put the shell of an oyster in the tea kettle and the lime will adhere to it instead of coating the sides.

---

43. *American Heritage Dictionary,* 2nd college ed., s.v. "copperas." Copperas is a greenish crystalline hydrated ferrous sulfate used in water purification.
44. *American Heritage Dictionary,* 2nd college ed., s.v. "cholera." Cholera is an acute, often fatal infectious epidemic disease caused by the microorganism *Vibro comma.*

- *To Clean Furniture*

To remove white spots from varnished furniture rub with a warm flannel dipped in spirits of turpentine.

Liquid for Cleaning Brass

Forty drops oil of vitriol[45] in 1 pint water; scrape a piece of rotten-stone[46] about 3 inches square into it.

To Clean Window Glasses

Take finely pulverized indigo.[47] Dip into it a linen rag moistened in vinegar wine or water and apply it briskly to the glass. Wipe off and polish with a dry cloth.

Cleaning Windows

The finest article for washing windows is deer skin as no particles come off to adhere to the glass and make it look as if washed with leather. There is no need of anything larger than a hand basin for washing windows. Wipe the glass first with the wet cloth or leather and after it has become dry with the clean cloth.

Candles and Nightlights

Lard Candles

To 12 lbs lard take 1 lb saltpetre[48] to make a sauce. Mix and pulverize. Dissolve in a gill of boiling water; pour in the lard before it is quite melted.

---

45. *American Heritage Dictionary*, 2nd college ed., s.v. "vitriol." Oil of vitriol is sulfuric acid.
46. George Macdonald Hocking, *A Dictionary of Terms in Pharmacognosy and Other Divisions of Economic Botany* (Springfield, Ill.: Charles C. Thomas, Publisher, 1955), s.v. "rottenstone." Rottenstone is a friable siliceous stone derived from limestone and used for polishing, as an abrasive.
47. Hocking, *Pharmacognosy*, s.v. "indigo." The extract of indigo is sodium indigotin disulfonate.
48. *American Heritage Dictionary*, 2nd college ed., s.v. "saltpeter." Saltpeter is potassium nitrate or sodium nitrate.

Stir the whole till it boils; skim off what rises. Simmer till the water is boiled out or till it ceases to throw out steam. Pour off the lard as soon as it's done and clean the pot while hot.

- *To Make Mutton Suet Candles in Imitation of Wax*

Throw quick lime in melted mutton suet; the lime will fall to the bottom and carry along with it all the dirt of the suet so as to leave it as pure and as fine as wax itself. Now if to one part of the suet you mix three of real wax you will have a very fine and to appearances a real wax.

Nightlights

Make a fine cotton and wax it and cut into the requisite length. Melt the grease, candle ends; fix the cotton in the middle of the pill boxes and pour in the grease which would be the better for adding some wax. Put to burn in a saucer with a 16th of an inch of water around the base of night light.

Nightlights Brodeuse

Dry some horse chestnuts. Skin and pierce them with little holes with a piercer. Let them steep in lamp oil for 24 hours. Then put a wick or match in one of the holes. Put the chestnut in a glass full of water. It will burn all night.

Insect Repellents

To Destroy Bugs

Take ¼ portion oil of Turpentine[49] and with a brush rub places infested. If in great numbers do so several times.

---

49. *American Heritage Dictionary,* 2nd college ed., s.v. "turpentine." Turpentine is a thin, volatile essential oil, obtained by steam distillation from the wood of pine trees and used as a paint thinner and medicinally as a liniment.

To Destroy Crickets

Put Scotch snuff upon their holes. Cockroaches may be banished by red wafers. Paint is destructive to all insects and so is lime.

To Expel Mosquitoes

Burn camphor in a room.

For Bed Bugs

Apply kerosene oil.

• Fleas, Bed Bugs

A writer in the *Gardener's Chronicle* recommends the use of oil of wormwood[50] to keep off the insects above named. Put a few drops on a handkerchief or piece of folded muslin and put in the bed haunted by the enemy.

• Bed Bug Poison

An ounce of quicksilver,[51] beat up with the white of two eggs and put on with a feather is the cleanest and surest bed bug poison.

• To Destroy Ants

It happened that a piece of camphor[52] was laid in a drawer containing sugar which was infested by ants. On opening it a few days afterwards the bottom of the drawer was strewn with ants. The experiment was repeated with success.

---

50. *American Heritage Dictionary,* 2nd college ed., s.v. "wormwood." Wormwood is an aromatic plant yielding a bitter extract used in making absinthe.
51. *American Heritage Dictionary,* 2nd college ed., s.v. "quicksilver." Quicksilver is mercury.
52. *American Heritage Dictionary,* 2nd college ed., s.v. "camphor." Camphor is a volatile crystalline compound obtained from camphor tree wood and used as an insect repellent.

To Keep Out Moths

Pack with your woolens small switches or branches recently broken from cedar trees.

To Drive Away Rats, Mrs. Gaillard

Pound up Potash and strew around the holes; throw some under the holes and rub on the side of the boards and under part where they come through.

To Expel Rats

Scatter a few leaves and stalks of willow in their paths.

To Expel Ants

Procure a large sponge; wash it well; press it very dry; by so doing it will leave the small cells open; lay it on the shelf where they are most troublesome; sprinkle some white sugar lightly over it 2 or 3 times a day and take a bucket of hot water to where the sponge is; carefully drop the sponge into the boiling water and you will slay them by thousands; squeeze the sponge and begin again.

Inks, Dyes, and Pastes

Cheap and Excellent Ink

Take ½ oz of extract of logwood,[53] and 10 grains of bichromate of potash[54] and dissolve them in a quart of hot rain water. When cold pour it into a glass bottle and leave it uncorked for a week or two. Exposure to the air is indispensable. It is better to get an oz of each as it is only 3 cts an oz.

---

53. *American Heritage Dictionary*, 2nd college ed., s.v. "logwood." Logwood is a tropical American tree having dark heartwood from which dye is made.
54. *American Heritage Dictionary*, 2nd college ed., s.v. "potash." Potash is potassium carbonate.

To Take Ink From a Floor

Cover the spot with fresh wood ashes. Wet a little. Let it remain 48 hours, keeping damp. Also good for linen or white cotton goods.

- *Ink Stains*

Editors of the *New York World:* In a visit to Marseilles, a little incident came within my observation which may prove serviceable to many of your large class of readers. In the Hotel Des Empereurs where I was residing, an inkstand was accidentally overturned upon a beautiful tablespread; those present thought that the cloth was ruined. A Servant being called in to remove the article from the table all were surprised when he assured us that no harm had been done, and more surprised still at witnessing the successful means resorted to for removing the ink stains. The servant sprinkled over the cloth a quantity of pepper and salt and rubbed them over its surface. The mixture soon absorbed every portion of the ink, and the table spread was in as good a condition as before the accident. The spread was of woolen fabric. I have never had any occasion for testing the merits of this simple mixture when applied to other cloths but it certainly would not be attended with any bad result.

Ink Stains

Ink stains may be removed from linen by dipping the part in hot melted tallow. A molded candle will do but a composite will not.

Cheap, but Good Blacking

To a teacup of molasses stir in lampblack[55] until it is thick. Then add the whites of two eggs well beaten and to this add a pint of vinegar or whiskey, and put in a bottle for use. Shake it before using.

---

55. *American Heritage Dictionary,* 2nd college ed., s.v. "lampblack." Lampblack is a gray or black pigment made from the soot collected from incompletely burned carbonaceous materials and is used as a pigment and in matches, explosives, and fertilizers.

A Cheap Dye

A gentleman has handed us a specimen of cotton yarn colored to represent copperas[56] which it does very closely. The dye employed is very cheap. It is made of red or black oak bark, the rough outside of which should be first trimmed off. Make a strong concoction of the bark by boiling, and to a pot of about ten gallons add a tablespoon of blue vitriol. The yarn to be colored should be put in and boiled for an hour or two and then washed as much as you please. The color will stand and the yarn will be found soft and free from the harshness usual in copperas dye.

• Paste That Is Paste

Dissolve an ounce of alum in a quart of warm water; and when cold add as much flour as will make it the consistency of cream, then stew into it as much powdered rosin as will stand on a shilling and two or three cloves; boil it to a consistency stirring all the time. It will keep for twelve months and when dry may be softened with water.

Liquid Glues

Dissolve common glue in just enough water to dissolve the glue into a liquid form. Remove from the fire and pour in enough alcohol to bring to a slight consistency, stirring briskly. Keep in a bottle with a piece of India rubber or Bladder over the mouth. In very cold weather warm a little.

Miscellaneous Formulas

Feather Stitch Knitting

Purl 2 clips and bind; knit two plain throw threads forward; Knit 1 throw thread forward and Knit 2 purl 2 together; repeat.

---

56. *American Heritage Dictionary*, 2nd college ed., s.v. "copperas." Copperas is a greenish, crystalline, hydrated ferrous sulfate used in the manufacture of inks and in water purification.

Cypress Vine to Plant

At night put your seeds in a cup and pour scalding water enough on to cover; soak until morning, then plant ¹/₂ an inch thick in light rich loam. Cover the spot with a piece of board which must not be removed until 48 hours after planting.

To Remove a Tight Stopper

Apply a cloth wetted in hot water to the neck of the bottle; the glass will then expand and allow the easy withdrawal of the stopper.

Copying Ferns

The most perfect and beautiful copies imaginable of ferns may be made by thoroughly saturating them in common porter[57] and then laying them flat between white sheets of paper, more pressure than of an ordinary book, and let them dry out.

❦ MEDICAL REMEDIES ❧
Stomach Complaints

NutGalls, Dr. Meigs

Best Galls, powdered[58]	¹/₂ oz
Cinnamon, powdered	2 drachm
Ginger	¹/₂ drachm
Best French Brandy	¹/₂ Pint

---

57. *American Heritage Dictionary,* 2nd college ed., s.v. "porter." Porter is dark beer made from malt that has been charred by drying at a high temperature.
58. Hocking, *Pharmacognosy,* s.v. "gall." A gall is the excrescences on twigs of a Levantine oak valued for its tannin content.

Stir well; let stand 2 hours in a warm place. Set fire to the Brandy and let it burn out holding in the flame several lumps of white sugar; Strain through coarse blotting paper. Take 20 to 30 drops in a little water 3 or 4 times a day. For simple diarrhea of children.

For Dysentery[59]

One tablespoon common salt, mixed with 2 tablespoon vinegar. Pour upon it ½ pt hot water. To be taken cool. 1 Wine glassful of this mixture taken every ½ hours. If nauseated take every hour. For a child the proportions are 1 tsp salt and 1 of vinegar in a tea cup water.

- ## Cure for Dysentery

A friend writing as follows from Columbus Ga., says I have been using persimmon syrup for ten years past for dysentery, and am persuaded that it has no equal as a remedy for that troublesome disease. It is a simple harmless and effectual astringent. It is made of persimmons before they are quite ripe. They should be mashed up put into boiling water and then strained through a coarse cloth. This rough juice may be preserved in sugar or syrup. If our soldiers in camp would adopt this remedy many long cases of chronic dysentery might be prevented.

For Diarrhea

Take a freshly killed chicken. Boil in 2 or 3 qts water for several hours and drink the broth freely. Or Take equal parts syrup rhubarb, paregoric and camphor. Mix. Dose for an adult 1 teaspoonful every 2 or 3 hours.

---

59. Theresa A. Singleton, *The Archaeology of Slavery and Plantation Life* (Orlando: Academic Press, Inc., 1985), pp. 180–81. The average age for both planters and salves in the nineteenth century was the fourth decade. Slaves, relying largely on cornmeal for food, suffered dietary deficiencies, infection, and parasitism. "The dietary malabsorption problems and systematic drain from parasite infestation are well known. Bacillary and amoebic infections also probably contributed to the death rate through diarrhea and dysentery for both elite and slave groups." Given these facts, it is not surprising that Emily had seven formulas for dealing with both diarrhea and dysentery.

Blackberry Cordial for Diarrhea

To 1/2 a bushel well mashed blackberries add 1/4 lb Allspice, 2 oz cinnamon, 2 oz cloves. Pulverize well, mix. Boil slowly till well done. Then strain or squeeze the juice thru homespun or flannel and add to each pt of juice 1 lb loaf sugar. Boil again, take off and while cooling add 1/2 a gallon best cognac brandy. Dose for an adult 1/2 a gill to a gill. For a child a tsp or more according to age.

For Diarrhea, For Cholic

A Teaspoon Salt; The same dissolved in a pint of cold water and go to bed.

Diarrhea

Three tablespoons Fennel seed, 2 oz soot from a wood fire, a dessert spoon of powdered Rhubard. Boil these in a pint of water down to a half pint. When cold, add a wine glass of brandy and sweeten with loaf sugar. Boil in a piece of cinnamon as long as your finger. Three or 4 times a day for an infant, a teaspoon. Mother adds a little gum Arabic and crabs eyes to the above.

Respiratory Complaints

For Croup

Take a piece of fresh lard the size of a butternut, rub it up with sugar as you would butter for pudding Sauce. Divide into 3 parts and give at intervals of 20 minutes.

Dr. Morris' Prescription for Whooping Cough

Carb Potass, 7 oz; Cocci, 8 oz; Sacch alb, 2; Aqua.
Dose: a dessert spoonful 3 times daily for a child a year old.

To Cure Cough

Dissolve 1 scruple salt of tartaric[60] in a $\frac{1}{4}$ pt water add 10 grams cochineal.[61] Sweeten. Give an infant $\frac{1}{4}$ tablesp 4 times a day; 2 years $\frac{1}{2}$ a tablesp; from 4 years a tablespoonful.

• For a Cough

Procure a small quantity of Peruvian bark[62] at a chemists where you have reasons to believe a genuine article may be obtained and on the very first symptoms of irritation of the throat and disposition towards what is termed hacking chew a piece about the size of a bean; this will at once relieve; and on recurrence of the symptoms apply the same remedy. By always keeping a piece in my pocket I have throughout this winter prevented a cough from proceeding beyond a day's growth, though I have been much exposed to the weather and evening air.

• To Stop Coughing

A correspondent of the *London Medical Gazette* states that to close the nostril with the thumb and finger during expiration leaving them open during inspiration will relieve a fit of coughing in a short time.

---

60. *American Heritage Dictionary,* 2nd college ed., s.v. "tartaric acid." Tartaric acid was employed medicinally, as in seidlitz powder.
61. *American Heritage Dictionary,* 2nd college ed., s.v. "cochineal." Cochineal is a brilliant red dye made by drying and pulverizing the bodies of females of the genus *Daactylopius coccus,* a tropical American scale insect that feeds on cacti.
62. *American Heritage Dictionary,* 2nd college ed., s.v. "Peruvian." Peruvian bark is the cinchona tree of South America whose bark yields quinine and other medicinal alkaloids.

Remedy for a Cough

Divide 1 pt water, in one half; dissolve 1 oz Rock Candy; in the other $\frac{1}{2}$ oz gum Arabic;[63] strain and add 1 oz Paregoric[64] and $2\frac{1}{2}$ oz Antimonial Wine.[65] Dose: 1 tbspf morning and evening for an adult, 1 dessert spoon for a child and 1 teasp for an infant. When the cough is troublesome give more frequently.

Certain Cure for Sore Throat

A poultice of wormwood[66] boiled in sweet milk and applied to the throat. Relief of most forms in 8 hours.

Flaxseed Syrup

Boil 1 oz flaxseed[67] in 1 qt water for $\frac{1}{2}$ an hour. Strain and add to the liquid the juice of 2 lemons and $\frac{1}{2}$ lb rock candy, 12 oz of powder gum Arabic can be added. Simmer for $\frac{1}{2}$ an hour stirring occasionally. Take a glass full when the cough is troublesome.

---

63. Hocking, *Pharmacognosy*, s.v. "gum arabic." Gum arabic is an amorphous substance derived from plants through disintegration of internal plant tissues and ordinarily exuding through the bark. This substance swells in water to form a gel or dissolves to form a colloidal dispersal; it consists of glycosidal acids combined with calcium, potassium, or magnesium.
64. *American Heritage Dictionary*, 2nd college ed., s.v. "paregoric." Paregoric is camphorated tincture of opium taken internally for the relief of diarrhea.
65. *American Heritage Dictionary*, 2nd college ed., s.v. "antimonial." Antimonial is a medicine with antimony as an ingredient. An antimony is a metallic element having four allotropic forms, the most common of which is a hard, brittle, lustrous silver-white crystalline material. Tartar emetic was an antimonial and was used to cause vomiting.
66. *American Heritage Dictionary*, 2nd college ed., s.v. "wormwood." Wormwood is any of several aromatic plants of the genus *Artemisia* native to Europe yielding a bitter extract used in making absinthe.
67. *American Heritage Dictionary*, 2nd college ed., s.v. "flaxseed." Flaxseed is the seed of flax and the source of linseed oil, used as an emollient in medicinal preparations.

Bread Jelly for the Sick

Take a penny roll, pare off the crust and cut the crumb in three slices; toast them lightly on both sides; put into a quart of spring water; simmer gently on the fire until the liquid becomes a jelly; strain through a thick cloth and flavor with a little lemon juice and sugar, added when hot. A glass of wine is an improvement. The jelly is very nourishing.

For Cold with Fever in Children

Calomel or mercury and chalk, ½ grams;[68] Rhubarb 1 oz.; Soda 1 oz.; Ipecac ¼ grams. The above each in powder. Give one every four hours in a little syrup till a laxative effect is produced then employ quinine if the fever continues. Sweet spirits of nitre and paregoric may be given at night. Mustard applications morning and evening.

Colds of the Head

May it is said be cured by inhaling Hartshorn.[69] The inhalation by the nose should be 7 or 8 times in 5 minutes.

• A Bad Cold

A bad cold like measles or mumps or other similar ailments, will run its course of about ten days in spite of what may be done for it unless remedial means are employed within forty-eight hours of its inception.

---

68. John S. Haller Jr., *American Medicine in Transition, 1840–1950* (Urbana: University of Illinois Press, 1981), p. 82. Calomel was a mercurous chloride that was used as a cathartic. It was prescribed as an antisyphilitic, diuretic, and antiseptic and produced serious results such as salivation, ulceration of the mouth, sloughing of the gum, and necrosis of the lower jaw, all a form of mercurial poisoning.

69. Hocking, *Pharmacognosy*, s.v. "hartshorn." Hartshorn is ammonia water or ammonium carbonate. It was a precursor of today's baking powder and baking soda.

Following is a short and safe way to cut a cold short. On the first day of taking a cold there is a very unpleasant sensation of chilliness. The moment you observe this go to your room and stay there; keep it at such a temperature as will entirely prevent this chilly feeling even if it requires a hundred degrees of Fahrenheit. In addition put your feet in water half leg deep as hot as you can bear it, adding hotter water from time to time for a quarter of an hour so that the water shall be hotter when you take your feet out than when you put them in it; then dry them thoroughly and put on warm thick woolen stockings even if it be summer for summer colds are the most dangerous; and for twenty-four hours eat not an atom of food but drink as largely as you desire of any kind of warm teas and at the end of that time if not sooner the cold will be effectually broken without any medicine whatever.

Cold in the Head

For a Cold in the head, fill a wash basin with boiling water; add 1 oz flour of mustard.[70] Then hold the head covered with a cloth to prevent the escape of steam over the basin.

Prescription for Sorethroat, Dr. Morris

Lemon piece fresh	2 oz
Bicarbonate potash[71]	5 Scruples[72]
Spring Water	2 oz

---

70. *American Heritage Dictionary*, 2nd college ed., s.v. "mustard." Flour of mustard is a powdered mustard seed used medicinally that may be made into a pastelike mixture with flour and water. The mustard seed is pungent and has been used in pickling, as a seasoning, and as the main ingredient in prepared mustard.

71. Hocking, *Pharmacognosy*, s.v. "potash." Potash is potassium chlorate, a chemical compound isolated in 1851.

72. *American Heritage Dictionary*, 2nd college ed., s.v. "scruple." A scruple is a unit of apothecary weight equal to about 1.3 grams or 20 grains.

SaltPetre[73]   12 grains
Make a Solution and give a teaspf every 2 hours (give more to adults).

- *Chloroform, A Remedy for Asthma*

The Medical Times relates a case of dry spasmodic asthma effectually cured by the inhalation of about fifteen measured drops of chloroform,[74] repeated as often as attacked. It has also it says been successful in a case of spasmodic croup.

- *Asthma*

A sufferer from asthma would record his gratitude by saying to his fellow sufferers that he has experienced an almost magical relief from the following simple remedy, viz: The leaves of the stramonium (or Jamestown weed[75]) dried in the shade, saturated with a pretty strong solution of saltpetre,[76] and smoked so as to inhale deeply the fumes. In order to inhale, fill the mouth with the smoke, then open the lips and draw in the breath. It may strangle at first if taken too freely, but it will loosen the grip that seems to spasm the breathing tubes, and bring up the sputum that settles in the bottom of the lungs.

- *Remedy for Congestive Chills*

The Mother of a soldier has sent to the *Petersburg Express* a remedy for congestive chills, which she has never known to fail. She has for a number

---

73. *American Heritage Dictionary*, 2nd college ed., s.v. "saltpeter." Saltpeter is composed of either potassium nitrate or sodium nitrate.

74. David L. Cowen and William H. Helfand, *Pharmacy, An Illustrated History* (New York: Harry N. Abrams, Inc., 1990), p. 125. Halogens included such chemical compounds as chlorine, iodine, and bromine. Chlorine early found medical and therapeutic uses in disinfectants and in chloroform.

75. *American Heritage Dictionary*, 2nd college ed., s.v. "James Town Weed." The Jimson weed of James Town weed is a coarse, poisonous plant having large, trumpet-shaped white or purplish flowers and prickly fruit.

76. *American Heritage Dictionary*, 2nd college ed., s.v. "saltpetre." Saltpetre is potassium nitrate or sodium nitrate.

of years been managing a large boarding school and has had some experience in nursing. The remedy is spirits of turpentine.[77] Give from 2 to 15 drops in syrup or toddy, rub the chest and extremities well adding a small quantity of oil of turpentine to prevent blistering. The extremities should be rubbed until reaction takes place. A cloth saturated with the mixture should be applied to the chest.

- *A New Remedy for Consumption*

Dr. Desmartes of Bordeaux has published in the *Abeille Medicale* the result of four years experience in reference to the curative effects of the sap of the pine tree on consumption. One instance quoted is of a young lady whose father, mother, sister, and other relations had all died of the disorder. She was afflicted with violent retching and spitting of blood, and all the symptoms of an advanced pulmonary consumption were ascertained by auscultation. The spitting of blood was stopped by administering one drachma of powdered rue[78] per day. Dr. Desmartes considers rue, Ruta Graveolens, to be one of the best hemostatics known. After which the patient took a bottle of pine sap per day for the space of two months and a half; at the end of which time every alarming symptom had disappeared. The patient suffered no relapse. He quotes many other instances. Pine sap usually purges in the beginning but this effect which is purely eliminative soon ceases.

Fevers

- *No use for Quinine, Editors of the Mississippian*

I beg to make public through the medium of your paper the following certain and thoroughly tried cure for ague and fever. One pint of cotton

---

77. *American Heritage Dictionary,* 2nd college ed., s.v. "turpentine." Turpentine is a thin, volatile oil obtained by steam distillation from the wood of pine trees and used medicinally as a liniment.

78. *American Heritage Dictionary,* 2nd college ed., s.v. "rue." Rue is an aromatic Eurasian plant of the genus *Ruta* having evergreen leaves that yield an acrid, volatile oil formerly used in medicine.

seed, two pints of water boiled down to one of tea taken warm one hour before the expected attack. Many persons will doubtless laugh at this simple remedy but I have tried it effectually and unhesitatingly say it is better than quinine and could I obtain the latter article at a dime a bottle, I would infinitely prefer the cotton seed tea.

- *Yellow Fever*

A correspondent of the *Bulletin* gives the following as a sure preventive of yellow fever. Having noticed Dr. Joxe's very appropriate suggestions relative to the treatment of yellow fever, I would also remark that dwelling houses and vessels may be protected from infection by the use of chlorine. This may be made by any one in the following manner. 1st Order a quantity of peroxide of manganese put up in papers of one ounce each. 2nd Mix the contents of one of these with five ounces of common salt stirring the two until thoroughly mixed. 3rd Take a glass funnel into a bottle and drop the above named mixture into it slowly so as not to choke the tube. 4th Measure half an ounce of sulphuric acid and add to it three ounces of water; 5th Pour this mixture into the bottle stopping it with a cork having a small hole bored through it, shake it moderately and let it stand in the room some two hours; then shake again and leave in another room. In this way every room can be disinfected.

- *Scarlet Fever*[79]

This disease is now very prevalent in this and the neighboring counties. A friend from Indiana county informs us that there are no less than thirty cases of it at the present time in the borough of Indiana. A gentleman who has tested the remedy in his own family gives us a certain preventive of

---

79. *American Heritage Dictionary*, 2nd college ed., s.v. "scarlet." Scarlet fever is an acute contagious disease caused by a hemolytic streptococcus and is characterized by a scarlet skin eruption and high fever.

this disease. Take a pint of pure rye whisky in which soak four or five cloves of garlic first bruising them so as to get the strength and give a teaspoonful before eating. Our friend who has tried it says he has never known it to fail. Where one member of the family has the fever the others by the use of this remedy have invariably escaped. *Pittsburgh Post.*

- *A Specific for Typhoid Fever*[80]

Editors of the *Nashville Union and American:* The generally received opinion that typhoid fever is a self limited disease and runs a certain course in spite of treatment is false. When I say this I know I say it in opposition to an opinion almost universally received and believed by physicians throughout the civilized world. The Iodide of Potassium[81] or the Iodide of Sodium in from three to five grain doses every six or eight hours, will always cure typhoid fever in about one week; unless there is an intercurrent disease to protract the fever. Never give Calomel[82] in well developed case: use laxatives if necessary, I often keep the bowels locked up three, five and sometimes eight or ten days. When you fail to check hemorrhage or even the running of the bowels, by ordinary means, inject cold water; the addition of a little Acetate of lead and Laudanum will make the injection much better. With the above as a main and other appropriate collateral treatments, I scarcely ever have much trouble with typhoid fever. I believe if every surgeon in the Southern Confederacy would adopt this treatment it would be the means of saving many a sweet life. S. Hinds, M.D.

---

80. *American Heritage Dictionary,* 2nd college ed., s.v. "typhoid." Typhoid fever is an acute, highly infectious disease caused by the typhoid bacillus, *Salmonella typhosa,* transmitted by contaminated food or water, and characterized by red rashes, high fever, bronchitis, and intestinal hemorrhaging.
81. *American Heritage Dictionary,* 2nd college ed., s.v. "iodide." An iodide is a binary compound of iodine with a more electropositive atom such as "Potassium."
82. *American Heritage Dictionary,* 2nd college ed., s.v. "calomel." Calomel is a white, tasteless compound used as a purgative. It was composed of mercurous chloride and had serious side effects, including mercurial poisoning.

Cure for Ague[83]

1 oz best powdered Rhubarb[84] and piece of Pearl Ash[85] size of a large nutmeg; pour on 1 pt boiling water stirring well. When cool bottle it. Dose: 1 tbspf before breakfast and the same an hour before dinner. Shake the bottle before taking it.

• *Camphorated Spirit*

At the present time of year there is always a great demand for camphor[86] in a liquid form. It is prepared as follows according to *Home Studies* by Rebecca Upton: Break gum camphor into bits until you have filled half a bottle then pour in alcohol. A few drops poured into a wine glass of water sometimes relieves faintness. If for external application you may fill the bottle with the best olive oil or Jamaica rum or whiskey. Camphor should not be drunk too frequently or to excess as it is apt to produce insanity. The solution affords relief when applied to bee or mosquito stings.

Camphorated Julip, Dr. Porcher

A ½ drachm camphor rubbed in a mortar with a lump of sugar and 1 scruple salt petre. Pour over these a pint of boiling water. When cold pour off, and add 2 teaspoons of spirits nitre, 1 antimonial wine. Excellent for fever or chilly sensations.

---

83. *American Heritage Dictionary,* 2nd college ed., s.v. "ague." Ague is a fever like that of malaria in which there are periods of chill, fever, and sweating.
84. *American Heritage Dictionary,* 2nd college ed., s.v. "rhubarb." The dried, bitter tasting rhizome and roots of rhubarb were used in Central Asia as a laxative.
85. Hocking, *Pharmacognosy,* s.v. "ash." Pearl ash is impure potassium carbonate.
86. *American Heritage Dictionary,* 2nd college ed., s.v. "camphor." Camphor is a volatile crystalline compound obtained from camphor tree wood.

• Poisons and Antidotes

It not infrequently happens that serious and distressing results are occasioned by the accidental employment of poison, and it occurred to us that we might possibly do a service to some of our readers by presenting them with a brief and compendious list of the more common poisons and the remedies for them most likely to be close at hand.

Acids: These cause great heat and sensation of burning pain from the mouth down to the stomach. Remedies: magnesia, soda, pearlash, or soap dissolved in water then use stomach pump or emetics.

Alcohol: First cleans out the stomach by an emetic, then dash cold water on the head, and give ammonia (spirits of hartshorn).

Alkalies: Best remedy is vinegar.

Ammonia: Remedy: lemon juice or vinegar, afterwards milk and water or flax seed tea.

Arsenic: Remedies: in the first place evacuate the stomach, then give the white of eggs, lime water or chalk and water, charcoal and the preparations of iron, particularly hydrate.

Belladonna or Night Henbane: Give emetics, and then plenty of vinegar and water or lemonade.

Charcoal: In poisons by carbonic gas, remove the patient to open air, dash cold water on the head and body, and stimulate nostrils and lungs by hartshorn, at the same time rubbing the chest briskly.

Corrosive Sublimate: Give white of eggs freshly mixed with water or give wheat flour and water, or soap and water freely.

Creosote: White of eggs and the emetics.

Laudanum: Same as opium.

Lead: White lead and sugar of lead. Remedies: alum, cathartic, such as castor oil and Epsom salts, especially.

Mushrooms, when poisonous: Give emetics and then plenty of vinegar and water with dose of ether if handy.

Nitrate of Potash, or Saltpetre: Give emetics, then copious draughts of flaxseed tea, milk and water and other soothing drinks.

Nitrate of Silver (lunar Caustic): Give a strong solution of common salt and then emetics.

Nux vomica: First emetics, then brandy.

Opium: First give a strong emetic of mustard and water; then strong coffee and acid drinks, dash cold water on the head.

Oxalic Acid: Frequently mistaken for Epsom salts. Remedies chalk, magnesia, or soap and water freely then emetics.

Prussic Acid: When there is time administer chlorine in the shape of soda or lime. Hot brandy and water. Hartshorn and turpentine also useful.

Snake bite: Apply immediately strong hartshorn and take it internally; also give sweet oil and stimulants freely apply a ligature tight above the part bitten and then apply a cupping glass.

Tartar Emetic: Give large doses of tea made of galls, Peruvian bark or white oak bark.

Tobacco: First an emetic, then astringent tea, then stimulants.

Verdigris: Plenty of white of egg and water.

White Vitrol: Give the patient plenty of milk and water.

In almost all cases of poisoning, emetics are highly useful and of those one of the very best because most prompt and ready is the common mustard flour or powder, a teaspoonful of which stirred up in warm water may be given every five or ten minutes until free vomiting can be obtained. Emetics and warm demulcent drinks such as milk and water, flax seed or slippery elm, tea, chalk, water, should be administered without delay. The subsequent management of the case will of course be left to a physician. Hartford Times

- *New Antidote for Strychnine*

Dr. Shaw of Texas has found sweet oil drunk freely a successful antidote to strychnine[87] in two cases. The oil is to be poured down without any reference to the patient's vomiting.

---

87. *American Heritage Dictionary,* 2nd college ed., s.v. "strychnine." Strychnine is an extremely poisonous white crystalline alkaloid derived from *Nux Vomica* and used as a poison for rodents and medicinally as a stimulant for the central nervous system. It is an important plant alkaloid.

Aches and Pains

- *Application of Chloroform*[88] in Neuralgia

The Edinburg Medical Journal contains an account by Dr. Little of his successful mode of applying chloroform in neuralgia. Dr. L's mode of application is to take a piece of lint a little less in size than the watch glass to be used, which need not be more than two inches in diameter, putting it on the hollow side of the glass, pouring on it a few drops of chloroform sufficient to saturate it and then applying it at once to the part affected, keeping the edges of the glass closely applied to the skin, by covering it with the hand for the purpose of keeping in position as well as of assisting the evaporation of the chloroform. This is done in from five to ten minutes according to the amount of irritation wished for. The patient, during this time will complain of the gradual increase of burning sensation not so severe as that produced by a mustard sinapism, which reaches its height in five minutes and then abates but does not entirely disappear for more than ten minutes. To insure the full operation of the remedy, it is necessary that the watch glass be rather concave and it be closely applied to the skin and that the hand applied over it be sensibly warm. The immediate effect of the application is to remove all local pain from neuralgia.

- *Cure for Neuralgia*[89]

Some time since we published at the request of a friend a recipe to cure neuralgia. Half a drachm of sal ammonia[90] in an ounce of camphor[91] water to be taken a teaspoonful at a dose and the dose repeated several

---

88. *American Heritage Dictionary*, 2nd college ed., s.v. "chloroform." Chloroform is a clear, colorless heavy liquid used as an anesthetic and comes from chlorine.
89. *American Heritage Dictionary*, 2nd college ed., s.v. "neuralgia." Neuralgia is a paroxysmal pain along a nerve.
90. *American Heritage Dictionary*, 2nd college ed., s.v. "ammonia." Sal ammonia is a form of ammonium hydroxide.
91. *American Heritage Dictionary*, 2nd college ed., s.v. "camphor." Camphor is a volatile crystalline compound obtained from camphor tree wood and used medicinally as a stimulant, expectorant, and diaphoretic.

times at intervals of five minutes if the pain be not relieved at once. Alta, California

For Toothache

Warm salt water held to the place.

Remedy for Toothache

To cure the toothache dissolve two drachmas of alum[92] in seven drachmas of sweet spirits of nitre;[93] a piece of lint or a small piece of sponge to be dipped in the solution and applied to the tooth.

• Remede Contre Les Maux Dents

On prend une cuiller a cafe de poudre de chasse, un morceau de mousseline fine, mais solide. On renferme la poudre dans la mousseline, on en forme un nouet que l'on ferme avec un fil bien cire. Au moment ou la douleur de dents se fait sentir, on met le nouet dans la bouche, on le mache; on expectere la salive qui se forme, et au bout d'heure la douleur disparait. Ce moyen est celui du fameux horloger de Saint Denis, qui a opere tant de guerisons.

Infections

• Tetanus[94] or Lockjaw

We have received the January number of *The New Orleans Medical and Surgical Journal,* A Hester, M.D. editor and proprietor. An article on the

---

92. *American Heritage Dictionary,* 2nd college ed., s.v. "alum." Alum is any of various double sulfates of a trivalent metal such as aluminum and a univalent metal such as potassium used medicinally as topical astringents and styptics.
93. Hocking, *Pharmacognosy,* s.v. "nitre." Sweet spirits of nitre is used in manufacturing soaps and shoe polishes and is poisonous.
94. *American Heritage Dictionary,* 2nd college ed., s.v. "tetanus." Tetanus is an acute, often fatal infectious disease caused by a bacillus, *Clostridium tetani,* that generally enters the body through wounds and is characterized by rigidity and spasmodic contraction of the voluntary muscles.

use of quinine[95] in Tetanus or lockjaw by E. A. Pye, M.D. of Louisiana is especially worthy of attention giving as it does the successful result of administering large doses of quinine in this we believe generally considered almost incurable disease. The patient was a negro boy residing in Cataboula Parish, La. about 14 years of age and laboring under a most violent attack of Traumatic Tetanus. He had it seems fallen from a horse some weeks previously, receiving a wound in the face. The wound was apparently slight, little attention was paid to it and it healed in the usual time. Symptoms of Tetanus however soon made their appearance and had gone on constantly from bad to worse in spite of the treatment. He had been purged, blistered, had taken opium, whisky, spirits of turpentine, calomel, the hot and cold bath but with no relief. At length it was determined to give quinine a trial and begin with 30 or 40 grams and increase the dose until some effects were produced. At this time the intervals between the paroxysms had dwindled to but a few moments of partial ease and with these transient exceptions the patient was in a state of constant and most violent episthotonos, and it was evident that unless relief could be procured death must soon close the terrible scene. Taking advantage of the first opportunity, the Doctor got down his throat 30 grains of quinine— examining his watch at the same time. In one hour he again visited him and perceiving no change repeated the dose. In the course of the next two hours the Doctor thought or fancied he perceived slight diminution in the intensity of the paroxysms; at any rate the boy thought himself relieved and begged for the medicine. He got 30 or 40 grains. The improvement in the next two hours was evident. The paroxysm were not only less severe but the interval was also decidedly longer and freer from pain. The boy's sensation of relief was yet more decided. The case went on regularly improving; the only other medicine given being an occasional dose of oil. At the end of two weeks the boy had taken two ounces of quinine; was entirely free from all symptoms of tetanus; had experienced no bad effect from this

---

95. *American Heritage Dictionary,* 2nd college ed., s.v. "quinine." Quinine is a bitter, colorless, amorphous powder or crystalline alkaloid derived from certain cinchona barks and used in medicine to treat malaria.

enormous quantity of quinine. The muscles had become relaxed, the skin was acting finely, the bowels were free. The only peculiar effect of the quinine being the feeling of the patient as if he were about half drunk or happy.

- *Puff Balls*[96] for Wounds

A writer who signs himself M.B.C. states that the common puff ball is perhaps the best possible application for a fresh cut or bleeding wound. Close the wound quickly as possible, break open the puff ball and apply it directly, tying it on; it will stop the bleeding almost or quite instantaneously, protect the wound like a cushion so that you can scarcely wet or hurt it and if the wound is not severe you have only to let it alone and it will be well almost before you are aware of it.

Cure for a Felon[97]

Equal parts of gum camphor and gum opium. Mix into a soap. Wet a paste with spirits Turpentine.

- *Whitlows*

Dr Guinier, professor of the Faculty of Medicine at Montpellier, has just published a letter in the *Abeille Medicale,* in which he describes a peculiar method employed by him for stopping the progress of a whitlow when in its first stage. A whitlow generally begins with a dull sensation of heat in the affected finger near the nail; a rose coloured spot of the size of a

---

96. *American Heritage Dictionary,* 2nd college ed., s.v. "puffball." A puffball is a fungus of the genus *Lycoperdon* having a ball-shaped fruiting body that when broken open releases the enclosed spores in puffs of dust.
97. *American Heritage Dictionary,* 2nd college ed., s.v. "felon." A felon is a suppurative infection involving the deep tissues on the palmar surface of the fingertips and was also called a whitlow.

lentil marks the seat of disease. This point when pressed is painful the colour disappears and immediately returns after the pressure has ceased. After the lapse of a few hours the pain becomes more permanent, the rose colour has become darker, and extends over a larger space while the skin becomes swollen. The pain increases rapidly but as yet without pulsation. This Dr. Guinier says is the proper time for applying his remedy. Having slightly wetted the inflamed surface he passes over the whole of it slowly with a pencil of lunar caustic[98] and he continues this operation for at least a minute in order to make sure that the influence of the caustic has penetrated through the cuticle. The moisture which has now become a concentrated solution of nitrate of silver is allowed to dry on the finger and completes the cauterisation. The skin soon becomes quite black, and the cure is then complete.

Odds and Ends

Sting of a Bee

In most cases relief can be obtained by pressing on the point stung with the tube of a key. This will extract the sting and relieve the pain and the application of spirits of Hartshorn.[99] A small quantity introduced into the wound on the point of a needle or fine nibbed pen and applied as soon as possible will scarcely ever fail.

To Remove Corns From Between the Toes

These corns are generally more painful than any others, and are frequently so situated as to be almost inaccessible to the usual remedies.

---

98. *American Heritage Dictionary,* 2nd college ed., s.v. "lunar." Lunar caustic is silver nitrate used in cauterization.
99. Hocking, *Pharmacognosy,* s.v. "hartshorn." Spirits of hartshorn is ammonia water.

Wetting them several times a day with hartshorn will in most cases cure them. Try it.

For Chapped Hands

After washing put 1 tsp glycerin in the palm and rub all over hands and wrist. Then dry.

To Remove Lumps in the Breast

Beat up a mallow apple and put on some as a poultice, changing it when hot and dry. Also sweet oil and Hartshorn on a bit of cloth.

• Cure for In Growing Nails

It is stated that cauterization by hot tallow is an immediate cure for in growing nails. Put a small piece of tallow in a spoon and heat it over a lamp until it becomes very hot and drop two or three drops between nail and granulatiors. The effect is almost magical. Pain and tenderness are at once relieved and in a few days the granulatiors all go leaving the diseased parts dry and destitute of all feeling and the edge of the nail exposed so as to admit of being pared away without any inconvenience. The operation causes little if any pain if the tallow is properly heated.

• Indigenous Medicinal Plants

The season having arrived for collecting many valuable indigenous medicinal plants, I propose to bring the subject before our Southern people, particularly our planters with the hope that they will not allow the time to pass without each one contributing his portion to an object so important to the health of our troops now fighting the battles of our country. Nor is the subject less important to us in a domestic point of view. Our planters now have it in their power not only to save money in the purchase of drugs but also to make the collecting and gathering of vegetable medicinal plants a source of income.

The Butterfly Weed or Pleurisy Root is a very common plant in South Carolina, growing in old fields and along the borders of meadows. Its brilliant clusters of bright scarlet flowers are well known to us as appearing in June and July. It is best collected in autumn. The root is the part used and is an excellent expectorant and diaphoric.

Puccoon or Blood Root, is a common plant throughout the Confederate States. Best collected in autumn but may be collected at any time. The root is the part used. It is emetic, expectorant and alternative.

Snake Root grows abundantly in the Southern country. It possesses emetic and cathartic properties is a valuable expectorant and is highly prized in chronic coughs, asthma and croup. It has been employed successfully in rheumatism and dropsy. The root is the part used.

Seneka Snake Root grows abundantly in the Southern country. It possesses emetic and cathartic properties, is a valuable expectorant, and is highly prized in chronic coughs, asthma and croup.

American Gentian, Blue Gentian or Samson Snake Root, is one of the purest tonics in the vegetable kingdom. It grows in grassy swamps and on the edges of roads and blossoms from September to December. It excites the appetite, invigorates the power of digestion and is much esteemed as a medicine in dyspepsia. The root is the part used and may be collected in Fall or Winter.

Canada Snake Root, Wild Ginger. This plant is found in woods and shady places, as far South as Carolina. It is aromatic, stimulant and tonic, and may be well employed as a substitute for ginger, all parts of the plant have a grateful aromatic odour, and more powerful in the root which is the part used. It also possesses diaphoretic properties,[100] and is sometimes used by the country people as a substitute for ginger. It is an admirable adjunct to tonic infusions and decoctions. It should now be collected.

Celamus, Sweet Flag. Found throughout the Confederate States, in low, wet, swampy places—it is aromatic and a stimulant tonic, and is used with great advantage in pain or uneasiness in the stomach or bowels, aris-

---

100. *American Heritage Dictionary,* 2nd college ed., s.v. "diaphoresis." Diaphoresis is perspiration when copious and medically induced.

ing from flatulency and in torpor or debility of the alimentary canal. The root is the part used.

Queen's Delight, or Queen's Root is a medicine of considerable value in scrofula, cutaneous, chronic hepatic affections and secondary syphillis. It grows abundantly in pine barrens, from Virginia to Florida. It is alterative. The root is the part used and should be collected late in the fall or early winter months. Pink Root, Carolina Pink. Grows abundantly throughout the Southern and Southwestern States. It is one of our most powerful enthemintics or worm medicine. Combined with senna it is the medicine of great value. The root is the part used and should be collected in the spring and fall months.

The Poke, commonly called weed, grows abundantly throughout the Confederate States along fences, by the borders of woods, and in newly cleared and uncultivated fields. It is emetic, slightly narcotic, and occasionally cathartic. It is also alternative and is highly recommended in rheumatic affections and syphillis. Ointments used in itch and other cutaneous diseases. Root is the part used and should be dug late in autumn or during the winter. Cut in transverse slices and dried. *MEDICUS*

Sea Sickness

Generally allow the stomach to discharge its contents once or twice and then if there is no organic disease give 5 drops of Chloroform in a little water and if necessary repeat the dose in 4 to 6 hours. Let the patient sleep and he will awake well.

• Remedy for Drunkenness

I would recommend ipecacuanha[101] as a remedy for drunkenness, taken in half drachm doses as an emetic. Ipecacuanha has the extraordinary

---

101. *American Heritage Dictionary,* 2nd college ed., s.v. "ipecacuanha." Ipecacuanha is a low-growing South American shrub having roots used medicinally. It is a cathartic and causes vomiting.

property of stimulating the whole system, equalizing the circulation, promoting the various secretions, and indeed, assisting each organ of the body in its function and to restore it to its normal state. Ipecacuanha can be taken with perfect safety as an emetic. I believe the administration of half a drachm of ipecacuanha as an emetic to be a cure of periodical drunkenness. It is observed that in the intervals between the periods of these attacks, the person is quite sober, and often remains so for two to four months or for a longer time. When the mania comes on, the intense desire for alcoholic stimulus is so strong as to render the sufferer subject to no control, and from the sensation of depression and sinking, he can look upon alcoholic stimulants as his only remedy. When a person is in this state, it will be always found that his stomach is in fault, and the unnatural appetite arises from that cause alone; if half a drachm of the powder of ipecacuanha be taken so as to produce full vomiting, the desire for intoxicating stimulants is immediately removed. Higginbottom.

- *The Cure of Drunkenness*

The irresistible passion for liquor which is acquired by men who cannot govern their appetites is quite as much a physical as a moral disease, and the terrible craving for the accustomed stimulus which constitutes the great the apparently irresistible obstacle to reform comes mostly from the local inflammation of the stomach and brain. Its cure by medical treatment is not therefore irrational and if it is possible it should be understood that those who struggle vainly to break the chains of a degrading habit may avail themselves of whatever medical reinforcement may contribute to the support of an enfeebled will. The receipt by which so many drunkards have been assisted to reform is as follows: Sulphate of iron, 5 grains; magnesia, 10 grains; peppermint water, 11 drachms; spirit of nutmeg, 1 drachm; twice a day. This preparation acts as a tonic and stimulant and so partially supplies the place of the accustomed liquor. *Springfield Republican*

For Hiccups

Take a piece brown paper; light, blow out; hold the fumes opposite the mouth and nose of the patient.

Cod Liver Oil[102]

The disagreeable taste of this oil may be masked by adding 10 percent common salt.

- *Cold Feet*

Cold feet are the avenues of death to multitudes every year; it is a sign of imperfect circulation and of want of vigor of constitution. No man can be well whose feet are habitually cold. When the blood is equally distributed to every part of the body there is general good health. If there be less blood at one point than is natural there is coldness and not only so there must be more than is natural at some other part of the system and then there is fever and that is unnatural heat or oppression. In the case of cold feet, the amount of blood wanting there collects at some other part of the body, which happens to be the weakest, to be the least able to throw up a barricade against the approaching enemy. Hence, when the lungs are weakest, the extra blood gathers there in the shape of a common cold or spitting blood. Clergymen, public speakers, and singers, by improper exposures, often render the throat the weakest part; to such persons cold feet gives hoarseness or a raw burning feeling. If you are well let yourself alone. But to those whose feet are inclined to be cold we suggest that as soon as you get up in the morning you put both your feet at once into a basin of cold water so as to come half way to the ankles; keep them in half a minute in winter a minute or two in summer rubbing them vigorously—wipe dry and hold to the fire in cold weather, until every part of the feet feel as dry as your hand then put on stockings. On going to bed at night hold your feet to the fire for ten or fifteen minutes until perfectly dry and get into bed. This is a most pleasant operation and fully repays for the trouble of it. No one can sleep well

---

102. *American Heritage Dictionary,* 2nd college ed., s.v. "cod." Cod liver oil is obtained from the liver of cod and contains a rich supply of vitamins A and D.

or refreshingly with cold feet. All Indians and hunters sleep with their feet to the fire. *Hall's Journal*

- *To Bring the Dead to Life*

To bring the dead to life immediately, as the body is removed from the water, press the chest suddenly and forcibly, downward and backward and instantly discontinue the pressure. Repeat this without interruption, until a pair of common hand bellows can be procured. When obtained, introduce the nozzle well upon the base of the tongue. Surround the mouth with a towel or handkerchief and close it. Direct a bystander to press firmly on the projecting part of the neck (called Adam's apple) and use the bellows actively. Then press upon the chest to expel the air from the lungs, to imitate natural breathing. Continue this at least an hour unless signs of natural breathing come on. Wrap the body in blankets and place it near a fire and do every thing to preserve the natural warmth as well as to impart an artificial heat if possible. Everything is secondary to inflating the lungs. Send for a medical man immediately. Avoid all frictions until respiration shall be in some degree restored.

Hot Water

Hot water is very efficacious for bruises or burns.

Twigg's Celebrated Hair Dye

Lac sulphur, 1 drachma; Sugar Lead, 2½ drachma; Rosewater,[103] 4 ounces. Shake and let it stand before using. Sulphurec of Potash is a superior hair dye; dissolve a little on the end of a knife in a little Rosewater. This is cheapest.

---

103. *American Heritage Dictionary,* 2nd college ed., s.v. "rose water." Rose water is a fragrant preparation made by steeping or distilling rose petals in water and is used in cosmetics.

Hair Wash

Take 1 oz Castor Oil;[104] mix thoroughly with 1 pt alcohol; add ½ oz tincture cantharides.[105] Brush the hair briskly with a hard brush; apply the lotion with a sponge. Wash the hair again. *Scientific American*

Hair Wash

For strengthening the hair, take 1 oz lac sulphur and ½ oz sugar of lead;[106] put in a bottle and pour on it a quart of Rosewater. Shake and let it stand for 2 or 3 days. Wash the whole head about twice a week. Or 1 drachma lac sulphur ½ drachma sugar lead and 4 oz Rosewater.

• *Medical Uses of Salt*

In many cases of disordered stomach a teaspoonful of salt is a certain cure. In the violent internal aching termed cholic add a teaspoonful of salt to a pint of cold water drink it and go to bed; it is one of the speediest remedies known. The same will revive a person who seems almost dead from receiving a heavy fall. In an apoplectic fit no time should be lost in pouring down salt and water. If sufficient sensibility remain to allow of swallowing; if not the head must be sponged with cold water until the sense returns, when salt will completely restore the patient from the lethargy. In a fit the feet should be placed in warm water with mustard added and the legs briskly rubbed, all bandages removed from the neck, and a cool apartment procured if possible. In many cases of severe bleeding at the lungs and when other remedies failed Dr. Rush found that two teaspoonsful of salt completely stayed the blood. In case of a bite from a mad

104. *American Heritage Dictionary*, 2nd college ed., s.v. "castor." Castor oil is a colorless oil extracted from castor-oil plant seeds and used as a cathartic and a fine lubricant.
105. Hocking, *Pharmacognosy*, s.v. "canthredes." Canthredes is the plural of cantharis, which is a beetle used as an aphrodisiac.
106. *American Heritage Dictionary*, 2nd college ed., s.v. "lead." Sugar of lead is lead acetate.

dog wash the part with a strong brine for an hour and then bind on some salt with a rag. In toothache warm salt and water held to the part and removed two or three times will relieve it in most cases. If the gums be affected wash the mouth with brine. If the teeth be covered with tartar, wash them twice a day with salt and water. Salt will expel worms if used in food in a moderate degree and aids digestion but salt meat is injurious if used much.

Glossary

Alum is any of various double sulfates of a trivalent metal such as aluminum and a univalent metal such as potassium used medicinally as topical astringents and styptics. Alum was used in cooking as a hardening or clarifying agent.

Ague is a fever like that of malaria in which there are periods of chill, fever, and sweating.

Antimonial is a medicine with antimony as an ingredient. An antimony is a metallic element having four allotropic forms, the most common of which is a hard, brittle, lustrous silver-white crystalline material.

Antimonial wine was composed of tartar emetic and caused nausea, shock, and vomiting. It was used in croups and lung diseases.

Bannock is a traditional Scottish cake usually made of barley meal and oatmeal and served at high tea.

Borax is hydrated sodium borate and is used in the manufacture of glass and ceramics.

Bouilli is beef or any meat cooked in bouillon to make a stew.

Calomel is a white, tasteless compound used as a purgative in nineteenth-century medicine. It was composed of mercurous chloride and was prescribed for syphilis, as a tonic, in small does as a stimulant, and in large doses as a sedative. It produced serious side effects, including mercurial poisoning.

Camphor is a volatile crystalline compound obtained from camphor tree wood and used as an insect repellent, and medicinally as a stimulant, expectorant, and diaphoretic.

Canthredes is the plural of cantharis, which is a beetle used as an aphrodisiac and as a diuretic.

Caper is a small bud of a bush native to the Mediterranean that is sun-dried and then pickled in a vinegar brine.

161

Carbonate of soda is sodium carbonate that produces carbonated water.

Castor oil is a colorless oil extracted from castor-oil plant seeds and used as a cathartic and a fine lubricant.

Chloroform is a clear, colorless heavy liquid used as an anesthetic and comes from the chemical compound chlorine.

Cholera is an acute, often fatal infectious epidemic disease caused by the microorganism *Vibro comma.*

Cochineal is a brilliant red dye made by drying and pulverizing the bodies of the females of a tropical American scale insect of the genus *Daactylopius coccus,* which feeds on cacti.

Cod liver oil is obtained from the liver of cod and contains a rich supply of vitamins A and D.

Copperas is a greenish, crystalline, hydrated ferrous sulfate used in the manufacture of inks and in water purification.

Curry powder is a pulverized blend of up to twenty spices, herbs, and seeds. Among the most commonly used are cardamon, chilies, cinnamon, cloves, coriander, cumin, fennel seed, mace, nutmeg, pepper, poppy and sesame seeds, saffron, tamarind, and turmeric.

Diaphoresis is perspiration when copious and medically induced.

Felon is a suppurative infection involving the deep tissues on the palmar surface of the fingertips and was also called a whitlow.

Flaxseed is the seed of flax and the source of linseed oil, used as an emollient in medicinal preparations.

Gall is the excrescences on twigs of a Levantine oak valued for its tannin content.

Gentian root has been used as a tonic.

Ginger root has a flavor that is peppery and slightly sweet, and its aroma is pungent and spicy. It is used in many savory dishes and in baked goods. Most ginger comes from Jamaica.

Groundnuts are the nutlike tubers of a climbing vine, *Apios tuberosa.* They are also peanuts.

Gum arabic is an amorphous substance derived from plants through disintegration of internal plant tissues and ordinarily exuding through the bark. This substance swells in water to form a gel or dissolves to form a colloidal dispersal—it consists of glycosidal acids combined with calcium, potassium, or magnesium.

Hartshorn is ammonia water or ammonium carbonate.

Indian meal is a term for cornmeal.

Indigo is sodium indigotin disulfonate.

Iodide is a binary compound of iodine with a more electropositive atom, such as "Potassium."

Ipecacuanha is a low-growing South American shrub having roots used medicinally mainly as a cathartic or to cause vomiting.

Isinglass or **fish gelatin** is a tough, whitish translucent substance prepared from the bladder of the sturgeon cod. It is employed in the household in the preparation of jellies, blancmange, and similar desserts. Gelatin from animal tissue has, however, largely supplanted it in cookery.

Jimson weed or **James Town** weed is a coarse, poisonous plant having large, trumpet-shaped white or purplish flowers and prickly fruit.

Lampblack is a gray or black pigment made from the soot collected from incompletely burned carbonaceous materials and is used as a pigment and in matches, explosives, and fertilizers.

Logwood is a tropical American tree having dark heartwood from which dye is made.

Lunar caustic is silver nitrate used in cauterization.

Lye is potassium hydroxide and is obtained by leaching wood ashes.

Mace is the bright red membrane that covers the nutmeg seed. As the membrane is removed and dried it becomes a yellow-orange color.

Mango is the fruit of the mango tree that has a large seed surrounded by fragrant sweet flesh that is brilliant golden orange.

Mustard flour is a powdered mustard seed used medicinally that may be made into a pastelike mixture with flour and water.

Neuralgia is a paroxysmal pain along a nerve.

Nitre—sweet spirits of, is used in manufacturing soaps and shoe polishes and is poisonous.

Oil of vitriol is sulfuric acid.

Paregoric is camphorated tincture of opium taken internally for the relief of diarrhea.

Pearl ash is impure potassium carbonate. It was used in curing meat, in making soap, and by the Indians in leavening breads.

Peruvian bark is from the cinchona tree of South America whose bark yields quinine and other medicinal alkaloids.

Porter is dark beer made from malt that has been charred by drying at a high temperature.

Potash is potassium chlorate.

Puffball is a fungus of the genus *Lycoperdon* having a ball-shaped fruiting body that when broken open releases the enclosed spores in puffs of dust.

Quicksilver is mercury.

Quinine is a bitter, colorless, amorphous powder or crystalline alkaloid derived from certain cinchona barks and used in medicine to treat malaria and fevers.

Rhubarb is the dried, bitter-tasting rhizome and roots used in Central Asia as a laxative. It was often combined with calomel.

Rose water is a fragrant preparation made by steeping or distilling rose petals in water and is used in cosmetics.

Rosin is the sap of pine trees.

Rottenstone is a friable siliceous stone derived from limestone and used for polishing, as an abrasive.

Rue is an aromatic Eurasian plant of the genus *Ruta* having evergreen leaves that yield an acrid, volatile oil formerly used in medicine.

Sal ammonia is a form of ammonium hydroxide.

Saleratus or **soda saleratus** is one of the chief ingredients of all baking powder.

Sally Lunn is a rich sweet yeast bread brought to America from England.

Saltpeter (or **saltpetre**) is composed of either potassium nitrate or sodium nitrate.

Salts of tartar are derived from tartaric acid and are used in baking powders.

Scarlet fever is an acute contagious disease caused by a hemolytic streptococcus and is characterized by a scarlet skin eruption and high fever.

Scrapple is a Pennsylvania Dutch dish derived from finely chopped scraps of cooked pork mixed with cornmeal and seasonings and cooked into a mush that is then put into loaf pans and cut.

Scruple is a unit of apothecary weight equal to about 1.3 grams or 20 grains.

Sesame seed or **bene seed** was brought to America by African slaves. The tiny seed has a nutty, sweet flavor and is used in candy and in baked goods.

Spirits of hartshorn is ammonia water.

Strychnine is an extremely poisonous white crystalline alkaloid derived from *nux vomica* and used as a poison for rodents and medicinally as a stimulant for the central nervous system.

Sugar of lead is lead acetate.

Sweetbreads are the thymus glands of veal, young beef, lamb, and pork.

Tartaric acid is used to make cream of tartar and is used in effervescent beverages and baking powders and was employed medicinally, as in seidlitz powder. It is an important acid in wine-making.

Tetanus is an acute, often fatal infectious disease caused by a bacillus, *Clostridium tetani,* that generally enters the body through wounds, and it is characterized by rigidity and spasmodic contraction of the voluntary muscles.

Turpentine is a thin volatile essential oil, obtained by steam distillation from the wood of pine trees and used as a paint thinner, and medicinally as a liniment.

Typhoid fever is an acute, highly infectious disease caused by the typhoid bacillus, *Salmonella typhosa,* transmitted by contaminated food or water and characterized by red rashes, high fever, bronchitis, and intestinal hemorrhaging.

Unslaked lime is calcium oxide.

Weights: A gill is equal to 4 fl. oz.; a pint is equal to 16 fl. oz.; a wine glass is equal to 2 fl. oz.; a large or tablespoon is equal to ½ fl. oz.; 1 small or teaspoon is equal to ⅛ fl. oz. Likewise 1 lb. flour would be equal to 3¼ cups of flour, and 1 oz. flour would equal over 3 tablespoons.[107]

---

107. Mary Randolph, *The Virginia House-wife,* p. 298. Hess has done a superb job of translating weights and measures used in the early nineteenth century into today's equivalents.

Wormwood is any of several aromatic plants of the genus *Artemisia* native to Europe and yielding a bitter extract used in making absinthe. In the past wormwood was used as a medicinal herb for colds, stomach problems, and rheumatism. However, the oil is potentially poisonous.

Index to Part I:
Portrait of Emily Wharton Sinkler

Index to Part II: Receipt Book

178